Thomas Duffus Hardy

A Review of the Present State of the Shakespearian

Controversy

Thomas Duffus Hardy

A Review of the Present State of the Shakespearian Controversy

ISBN/EAN: 9783337061821

Printed in Europe, USA, Canada, Australia, Japan

Cover: Foto ©Thomas Meinert / pixelio.de

More available books at **www.hansebooks.com**

A REVIEW

OF THE

PRESENT STATE

OF THE

SHAKESPEARIAN CONTROVERSY.

BY THOMAS DUFFUS HARDY,
ASSISTANT KEEPER OF THE PUBLIC RECORDS.

LONDON:
LONGMAN, GREEN, LONGMAN, AND ROBERTS.
1860.

"I can have no right," says Mr. Collier in his reply to Mr. Hamilton's "Inquiry," "to complain that "if there be fair and reasonable ground for believing "that a fraud and imposture has been attempted "or committed, one department, or even all the "departments of our great national institution, "should step forward to guard the public against "the delusion. I look upon it, in fact, as part "of their duty; but they are bound to discharge "that duty with as much expedition as is com-"patible with a proper sifting of the case; and they "are bound, moreover, not only to limit themselves "in the execution of their task to what necessity "may require, but to proceed with due regard "to the character and dignity of their own position. "A dispassionate sobriety ought to be observed, "if merely for the sake of the effect to be "produced, and the whole inquiry ought to "be conducted with the utmost temper and "moderation."

If Mr. Collier had followed the precepts he has thus laid down, an important question, which to a certain extent may be said to concern the whole literature of England, would have been dispassionately discussed, and his opponents, if opponents they must be called, would have no reason to object

A

to the ungenerous insinuations with which his statements abound. Should Mr. Collier complain of the tone which has been adopted by those who differ from him in this matter, he has no one to blame but himself. It was the injudicious answer he sent to the " Times " newspaper, in reply to Mr. Hamilton's letter, that has caused him the annoyance, by making it a personal, rather than a literary, question.

Public Record Office,
   July 1860.

A REVIEW

OF THE

PRESENT STATE OF THE SHAKESPEARIAN CONTROVERSY.

A MOST important literary question has engaged public attention since last July. Not that it is new to those who take an interest in dramatic, and more especially Shakespearian, literature; for it has been before the world since January 1852, when Mr. Collier first announced, in the *Athenæum* that he had discovered in a copy of the second folio edition of Shakespeare's Plays, published in 1632, a large body of Notes and Emendations, amounting to nearly 20,000, in a hand not much later than the time when this edition emanated from the press, and that in his belief the Annotator had made these emendations from better authority than that of the Editors of the first folio.

This announcement naturally created a great desire on the part of Shakespearian critics, and other literary men, for a detailed account of these Notes and Emendations; and in order that any person interested in the subject might have an opportunity of inspecting them, Mr. Collier, as he states, exhibited the book before the Shakespearian Society, and, on three occasions, before the Society of Antiquaries. Further to gratify the curiosity that had then been raised, in the year 1852 Mr. Collier published a volume professing to contain the greater part, but not all, of these manuscript alterations, with a fac-simile of a portion of one page. No sooner had Mr. Collier made public some of the emendations of this annotated folio, than the most lively interest was excited, not only in England, but on the Continent as well. The new readings were, however, violently assailed by critics of every denomination ; one alone (Professor Mommsen) accepting them as genuine. In England, Mr. Singer, Mr. Dyce, Mr. Staunton, Mr. Hunter, and Mr. C. Knight repudiated them in no very measured terms. According to these gentlemen, they were not what they professed to be; the "Old Corrector" (as Mr. Collier termed their author) had no authority for his corrections; on the contrary, the greater part of them were adopted from recent annotators; those of which the original could not be traced were violent and inconsiderate changes for the worse; the larger number were frivolous and unnecessary.—Such was the gist of the allegations made in reference to these readings.

The scholars who thus impugned the genuineness of these emendations, arrived at their conclusions wholly from their knowledge of Shakespeare's text, and of what had been done for it by Commentators during the present century and the last. They had never examined Mr. Collier's folio, though more than one had endeavoured to obtain an opportunity of doing so. As early as 1853 Mr. Charles Knight pointed out, in a temperate but forcible manner, the propriety of having the folio deposited in the custody of some public body, who would allow access to it, under proper regulations, and a full and satisfactory examination of its contents. Disregarding, however, the adverse opinions thus expressed, Mr. Collier, in 1853, issued a Second Edition of the Notes and Emendations; and, shortly after, the folio became the property of the Duke of Devonshire. All further chance of a critical examination of the volume had now become apparently hopeless; and it was after a considerable lapse of time, that Mr. Howard Staunton determined, if possible, to have the handwriting in which these emendations were made examined. "Having myself," he remarks,[*] "from the first publication of the Notes and Emendations, felt assured, by the internal evidence, that they were for the most part plagiarized from the chief Shakespearian editors and critics, and the rest of quite modern fabrication, I earnestly longed to have the writing tested. That which was a desire before, when the present work was undertaken, became a necessity; and during the year 1858 I more than once communicated to Sir Frederick Madden, as the most eminent palæographer of the age, my motives for wishing that the volume should undergo inspection by persons skilled in ancient handwriting." Sir F. Madden's official engagements at that time prevented his giving the subject the attention it deserved; but in consequence of Mr. Staunton's

---

[*] Preface to his Edition of Shakespeare.

solicitations, Sir Frederick applied to Mr. Collier for his good services in obtaining access to the volume. To this application Mr. Collier made no reply; whereupon, Sir F. Madden requested of the Duke of Devonshire himself the loan of the volume for a short time, in order to afford Professor Bodenstedt, Mr. Staunton, and others an opportunity of inspecting it. These gentlemen, and others, who seem to have been perfectly familiar with the handwritings of the period in question, after careful examination were unanimously of opinion that the manuscript notes and emendations were modern fabrications, although written in imitation of hands of the seventeenth century. This opinion was communicated by Mr. N. E. S. A. Hamilton to the *Times* newspaper in a letter of the 22d June 1859 ; when he also pointed out the remarkable fact, that an infinite number of faint pencil-marks and corrections, written in a hand of the present century, could be seen on the margins of the book, and that some of these pencil-marks could be distinctly. traced underneath the ink of many of the emendations.

Mr. Collier, in his reply, also published in the *Times*, denied these assertions; and courted " the most minute, the most searching, and the most hostile examination of Mr. Hamilton's allegations."

We purpose, therefore, taking Mr. Collier at his word, to enter upon such an examination as he courts.—Not, however, in any hostile spirit, but with a sincere desire to ascertain the truth. The subject is too important and too grave to require or admit of personal recriminations.

As Mr. Collier rests the authority of his folio upon the antiquity of the handwriting in which those emendations are made, we purpose examining this claim to authority under the following heads:—

    I. Is the writing, in which the Notes and Emendations occur, of the period of which Mr. Collier alleges it to be ?

    II. Are there any pencillings in the margin, as Mr. Hamilton professes to have discovered ?

    III. Do the Notes and Emendations carry upon their face proofs of their genuineness ?

    IV. What is the history of the folio in which these Notes and Emendations are found ?

and lastly, on collateral grounds : —

> V. Are certain Letters and Papers relating to Shake-
> speare which Mr. Collier has printed, or referred
> to, genuine or not?

I. Is the writing, in which the notes and emendations occur, of the period of which Mr Collier alleges it to be?

It is almost impossible to convey to the mind of the uninitiated a correct notion of the shades of difference in the handwritings of the sixteenth and seventeenth centuries ; and yet a practised eye distinguishes at a glance one from another, as easily as a man who, finding half a dozen letters from intimate friends upon his table, can tell who are the writers without looking at the signatures, and yet would be at a loss to describe the different characteristics which enabled him to form his conclusion.

The handwriting of the notes and alterations in the Devonshire folio is of a mixed character, varying, even in the same page, from the stiff laboured Gothic hand of the sixteenth century to the round text-hand of the nineteenth, a fact most perceptible in the capital letters. It bears unequivocal marks also of laborious imitation through-out.

In their broader characteristics the features of the handwriting of this country, from the time of the Reformation, may be arranged under four epochs, sufficiently distinct to elucidate our argument : —

1. The stiff upright Gothic of Henry VIII. and Edward VI.

2. The same, inclining, and less stiff, as a greater amount of correspondence demanded an easier style of writing, under Elizabeth.

3. The cursive, based on an Italian model (the Gothic becoming more flexible and now rapidly disappearing), in the reign of James I., and continuing in use for about a century.

4. The round hand of the schoolmaster, under the House of Hanover, degenerating into the careless half-formed hands of the present day.

Now, it is perfectly possible, that any two of these hands in succession, may have been practised by the same person ; although hand-writings, with all their modifications, are far more stationary in their essential characteristics, than an inexperienced inquirer would generally suppose. That the first and third, or the second and fourth should be co-existent is very improbable. That all, or that the first, second, and fourth should be found together, as belonging to one and the same era, we hold to be utterly impossible.

Yet this is a difficulty that Mr. Collier has to explain ; as the hand-writings of the MS. corrections in the Devonshire folio, including those in pencil, vary, as already said, from the stiff, upright, laboured, and earlier Gothic to the round text-hand of the nineteenth century.

" But," says the *Edinburgh* Reviewer,* with considerable caution though he betrays the uncertainty of the ground on which he is venturing, " in many an instrument of the seventeenth century, engrossed in the Gothic, names of places and persons, and other words to which it was wished to attract special attention, were inserted in a cursive hand, very like modern handwriting in general appearance. Such a cursive an old Corrector may have used in his freer pencil jottings, to be replaced by elaborate half-printing in penmanship."

Now, the truth is, that the cursive hand of the seventeenth century is utterly unlike the cursive hand of these pencillings. It is so far from being like, that no practised eye could be deceived by it. The cursive hand of these Gothic instruments is of the most perfect and graceful kind. It was derived from the Italian scholars, and based on the type now named 'italic.' If the reader will refer to any works printed in italics in the 17th century, *e. g.* to Bacon's " Novum Organum," or his " De Augmentis," or, still better, to his MSS. preserved in the British Museum, he will be able to form a tolerably accurate conception of the nature of cursive writing in the 17th century ; a hand as distinct from the slovenly round text-hand of these pencillings as it is from the Gothic of an earlier period.

* No. 226, pp. 452–486.

The Reviewer might as well confound Norman with Pointed Architecture, or Batty Langley with Cinque Cento.

But the reason assigned by the Reviewer for the prevalence of the stiffer Gothic hand in the Shakespeare emendations is really extraordinary. The folio in which they are made appeared in 1632. We must allow some years to have elapsed before the Corrector had completed his labours. Mr. Collier assigns them to the Commonwealth. Assume the period to be 1650. The corrections, then, ought to have appeared in the prevalent writing of that era; that is, in the ordinary cursive hand of the period, or, it may be, in a hand a little more antiquated, supposing they were the work of a provincial; for handwriting, like manners, was in those times somewhat less in advance in the provinces than in the metropolis. Fac-similes of this hand are too common for any one to be at a loss to understand its general character. But, on turning to the corrections in the Devonshire folio, they are ostensibly in the hand of a much earlier date, *i.e.* of Queen Elizabeth or the earlier period of James I., while the pencillings are in a cursive hand of the 19th century. Supposing, however, for a moment that these pencillings had really been (what they are not) in a cursive hand with all the undeniable characteristics of the middle of the 17th century, what conceivable motive could the "old Corrector" have had in deliberately transforming them into a hand which had long gone out of fashion? It can hardly be supposed that it could be for his own convenience or pleasure that he undertook such an amount of unprofitable labour, for what was to be gained by it? Could it, then, be for the printer's use? Certainly not; though the corrections are made in the style of adapting a book for the press.

It is possible to conceive a reason for inverting the process, that is, for transforming Gothic pencil writing into ink cursive; but none whatever for the reverse. Had the pencil writing been in Gothic, and had the majority of the written corrections been in the prevalent hand of 1650, we could then have conceived that the writer, for the sake of clearness, had been transferring the less legible Gothic into the more legible cursive; but why he should undertake the task of replacing the distinct and modern by the indistinct and antiquated, passes our comprehension.

There is another consideration which, slight as it may appear, will not fail to have weight with those who have been accustomed to the study of handwriting in general. Mr. Collier avows his belief that all these corrections are by one and the same hand. Perhaps he is right; but, if so, how does he account for the extraordinary variations in the letters ? In the commonest capitals there are to be found as many as half a dozen different forms of the same letter; several of which appear to have been written at first in an ordinary modern character, and afterwards altered and retouched with the evident design of creating a more antique appearance. Let Mr. Collier, from the British Museum, or from the State Paper Office, furnish a single instance of one writer at any period who, in writing according to the usage of that period, has thus luxuriated in varying the form of his capitals.

We shall say only a few words on the subject of the material in which the corrections are made, as Mr. Maskelyne has given clear evidence that it is not what is commonly called the " black ink " in use at any period.

The pigment, or whatever else it may be, is of different shades, often varying on the same page from a yellow brown to a light Indian ink ; a fact that seems to show that the corrections were made at different times. This may have given rise to the supposition that they were made by different persons at long intervals of time; but it appears to us, from the peculiarities in the writing and the different shades of ink, that they were made by the same hand, though undoubtedly at different periods. Believing, as we do, that they have no claims to antiquity, but are in reality recent fabrications, our opinion is simply this : that whenever the " Old Corrector " has come across any reading suggested, or error corrected, by any of the Shakespearian scholars of the last century or the present that has at all taken his fancy, he has seized upon them and inserted them in the folio ; and that thus are the various shades of the ink to be accounted for. Chemical tests, if they were allowed to be tried, would at once determine what are the component parts of the liquid in which the corrections are written.

II. Are there any pencillings in the margin, as Mr. Hamilton professes to have discovered ?

It has been already stated that Mr. Hamilton, on examining the emendations, discovered in the margins a number of faint pencil-marks and corrections, written in a hand of the present century, and that some of these pencil-marks could be distinctly traced underneath the ink. This fact and other circumstances, singly of little importance, tend collectively to establish the charge of fabrication. On this point, too, there is other evidence than palæography ; and Mr. Maskelyne's testimony,* resting on independent grounds, cannot be lightly set aside.—" This simple test (the microscope) of the character of these emendations, I brought to bear on them, and with the following results :—

" Firstly. As to any question that might be raised concerning the presence of the pencil-marks asserted to be so plentifully distributed down the margin, the answer is, they are there. The microscope reveals the particles of plumbago in the hollows of the paper ; and in no case that I have yet examined, does it fail to bring this fact forward into incontrovertible reality.

" Secondly, the ink presents a rather singular aspect under the microscope. Its appearance in many cases on or rather in the paper suggested the idea of its being a water-colour paint rather than an ink ; it has a remarkable lustre, and the distribution of the particles of colouring matter in it seems unlike that in inks, ancient or modern, that I have yet examined.

" This view is somewhat confirmed by a taste, unlike the styptic taste of ordinary inks, which it imparts to the tongue, and by its substance evidently yielding to the action of damp. But on this point, as on another, to which attention will be presently drawn, it was not possible to arrive at a satisfactory conclusion in the absence of the Dúke of Devonshire's permission to make a few experiments on the volume.

" His Grace visited the Museum yesterday, and was good enough to give me his consent to this. The result has been, that the suspicions previously entertained regarding the ink were confirmed.

---

* Printed in Mr. Hamilton's *Inquiry*, p. 27–29.

" It proves to be a paint removable, with the exception of a slight stain, by mere water, while, on the other hand, its colouring matter resists the action of chymical agents which rapidly change inks, ancient or modern, whose colour is due to iron.   In some places, indeed, this paint seems to have become mixed, accidentally or otherwise, with ordinary ink ; but its prevailing character is that of a paint formed perhaps of sepia, or of sepia mixed with a little Indian ink. This, however, is of secondary importance in comparison with the other point which has been alluded to.   This point involves, indeed, the most important question that has arisen, and concerns the relative dates of the modern-looking pencil marks, and the old emendations of the text which are in ink.   The pencil marks are of different kinds.   Some are ᴕ's, indicative of the deletion of stops or letters in the text, and to which alterations in ink, I believe, invariably respond.   Others, again, belong to the various modes at present in use to indicate corrigenda for the press.   Some may, perhaps, be the ' crosses, ticks, or lines ' which Mr. Collier introduced himself.   But there are others, again, in which whole syllables or words in pencil are not so effectually rubbed out as not to be still traceable and legible, and even the character of the handwriting discernible, while in near neighbourhood to them the same syllable or word is repeated in the paint-like ink before described.   The pencil is in a modern-looking hand; the ink in a quaint antique-looking writing.   In several cases, however, the ink word and the pencil word occupy the same ground in the margin, and are one over the other.   The question that arises in these cases, of whether these two writings are both ancient or both modern, is a question for the antiquary or palæographist. The question of whether the pencil is antecedent or subsequent to the ink, is resolvable into a physical inquiry as to whether the ink overlies the pencil or the pencil is superposed upon the ink.   The answer to this question is as follows :—

" I have nowhere been able to detect the pencil-marks clearly overlying the ink, though in several places the pencil stops abruptly at the ink, and in some seems to be just traceable through its translucent substance, while lacking there the general metallic lustre of the plumbago.   But the question is set at rest by the removal by water of the ink in instances where the ink and the pencil intersected each other. The first case I chose for this was an *u* in *Richard II.*, p. 36.

A pencil tick crossed the *u*, intersecting each limb of the
letter. The pencil was barely visible through the first
stroke, and not at all visible under the second stroke of
the *u*. On damping off the ink in the first stroke, however, the pencil-mark became much plainer than before,
and even when as much of the ink stain as possible was
removed, and the pencil still runs through the ink in
unbroken continuity. Had the pencil been superposed on
the ink, it must have lain superficially upon its lustrous
surface, and have been removed in the washing. We must,
I think, be led by this inference that the pencil underlies
the ink, that is to say, was antecedent to it in its date ;
while also, it is evident that the ' old commentator' had
done his best to rub out the pencil writing before he
introduced its ink substitute."

To this evidence other considerations must be added :
the appearance of white spots in the paper, as if acids had
been used to delete the ink ; and the frequency of erasures by
penknife or wet cloth. All these cannot but be startling
facts to persons acquainted with ancient MSS., and would at
once raise a doubt of the genuineness of any document
where they occurred, more especially one alleged to belong
to the 17th century. If this statement be questioned, let
the believers in the genuineness of these emendations produce instances of such usages prevailing in the middle of the
17th century ; MSS. of that period are numerous enough.
No one can undertake to prove an universal negative ; but
until some positive proof has been given of the prevalence of
such practices as these, unusual and suspicious as they undoubtedly are, we cannot do otherwise than refuse our assent
to the arguments adduced in favour of the antiquity of the
emendations in the Devonshire folio.

Attempts have been made, and indeed very unjustly,
from the inadequacy of the fac-simile in Mr. Hamilton's
volume to imply the non-existence in reality of these pencil-
marks. Mr. Netherclift, senior, has taken upon himself the
superfluous task of informing the public that he did not
execute them. What inference he would have us to deduce
from this, it is difficult, perhaps impossible, to say ; but it
would have been more to the point if he could have shown
that these pencil-marks did not exist. On this point, however, we have the evidence of the " Old Corrector's " own
advocate, the *Edinburgh* Reviewer :—

" There they are (the pencil marks) most undoubtedly, and in very great number too. The natural surprise that they were not earlier detected, is somewhat diminished on inspection. Some say they have ' come out' more in the course of years; whether this is possible we know not. But even now they are hard to discover, until the eye has become used to the search. But when it has—especially with the aid of a glass at first—they become perceptible enough; words, ticks, points, and all. In many places even the most sceptical observer can hardly doubt that the mode of correction was, as alleged for the prosecution, by pencil first, and ink afterwards. And in others, where no pencilling can be read, there is an appearance as if it had been rubbed out. Are these pencillings in a modern hand? That, after all, is the real issue of this complicated case. And it is one which me must leave to better eyes and more experienced judges, whenever this unfortunate volume shall be honestly examined. For the vehement assertions of partisans we care nothing. All we can say is, that to our eyes the faint and feeble ghosts of words and letters which are here and there to be made out, do wear the appearance of a hand more like that now in use, than the stiff gothic ink writing. But then we must observe on the other hand, that even in Elizabeth's reign the mixture of cursive with Gothic was very common. In many an instrument of the seventeenth century engrossed in the Gothic, names of places and persons, and other words to which it was wished to attract special attention, were inserted in a cursive hand very like modern hand-writing in general appearance. Such a cursive an old corrector may have used in his freer pencil jottings, to be replaced by elaborate half-printing in penmanship. This, however, we can but give as conjecture. We must, at all events, utterly disclaim and repudiate Mr. Netherclift's fac-similes in Mr. Hamilton's volume, if they are intended to be verified by the naked eye or by an ordinary glass. They are to our view infinitely too distinct, and we have carefully compared each of them with the original. In particular we must caution our readers against the very modern-looking ' r ' in armed (cited as from Hamlet, p. 277, col. 1.) Our sight, at least, failed altogether to discover its counterpart in the Perkins volume."

The tortuous ingenuity displayed in this extract is worth observing. The Reviewer having inveighed, in the earlier portion of his remarks, against the current maxim, *Cuilibet in arte sua credendum*, now requires his readers to yield their judgment at discretion to his own notions upon palæography and his unsupported surmise. True, he has the modesty to say that he offers the explanation as his own conjecture; not the less, however, intending to have it accepted as all-sufficient in reference to these pencil-marks; an issue which he has the very moment before " left to better eyes and more experienced judges."

Again, a recent writer in the *Athenæum* (N° 1686) dismisses the question of the pencil-marks, because Mr. Netherclift's fac-simile represents them as more legible than they really are: a fault, in fact, which could hardly have been avoided. Had he exaggerated the forms of the letters, or drawn them more nearly resembling modern handwriting than they really do, the objection might have been to some purpose. But, in reality, the only question is the fact of their being there, not of their being more or less legible. Indeed the more distinct and legible they were, the more would they tell in favour of the volume; the less studied intention would they betray of having been obliterated to serve the purposes of conceal-ment.* The *Athenæum* states that no pencil-marks existed; and Mr. Collier has improved this apparent advantage by asserting that there were no such pencil-marks in the book while it was in his possession; apparently intending to imply that if there now are, they must have been inserted by the British Museum authorities, who are well acquainted with his handwriting. We will not insult the common sense or candour of the reader by comment on such a defence as this; but we must again call attention to the contradictory argu-ments employed by Mr. Collier's supporters in upholding his views and statements as to this volume. What Mr. Col-lier and the *Athenæum* deny to exist at all†,—what the Editor of *Notes and Queries* " cannot see,"— is perceptible enough to the *Edinburgh* Reviewer.

---

* Whatever may have been the origin or purpose of these pencil-marks, it is clear that some one has deemed it advisable that their traces and evidence should be destroyed as far as possible, and that great efforts had been made to obliterate them by rubbing out.

† Mr. Collier states that neither he nor the Duke of Devonshire ever dis-covered a single pencil-mark, and that another friend of his had the folio under his eyes for one week and examined every page of it, and never saw a single pencil-mark.

"There they are," he states, "most undoubtedly, and in very great number too." "In many places (he subjoins), the most sceptical observer can hardly doubt that the mode of correction was by pencil first and ink afterwards. And in others, where no pencilling can be read, there is an appearance as if it had been rubbed out."

Whatever the public may think of this admission Mr. Collier can hardly thank the writer for making it. The Reviewer continues: "All we can say is, that to our eyes, the faint and feeble ghosts of words and letters which are here and there to be made out, do wear the appearance of a hand more like that now in use than the stiff Gothic ink writing." The method by which he escapes the fatal conclusion is, at all events, novel. These pencillings do occur; "but then we must observe, on the other hand, that even in Elizabeth's reign the mixture of cursive with Gothic was very common."

What "experts" were at the elbow of the Reviewer when he put forth this novel discovery in palæography? It exhibits all the pomp and pretentiousness of sciolism, and, like most novelties, is equally false and flimsy. What have instruments *engrossed*, or *legal* documents, of the seventeenth century to do with annotations scribbled in the margin of a book, first in pencil, in a modern hand, and afterwards in ink, in a hand of a much earlier period? Because Gothic engrossing is to be found in legal documents of 1650, therefore he concludes that such hand was the ordinary hand of the Commonwealth. But what, it may be further asked, has the mixture of cursive and Gothic in the time of Elizabeth to do with the handwriting of 1650? and even if it had, what has it to do with pencillings which wear all the appearance of a hand of the present century? The juxtaposition of the Reviewer's sentences looks very much like a studied attempt to mislead the unwary. Without any logical connexion, they carry the appearance of such connexion to the mind of the inexperienced reader. The Reviewer wishes to show that engrossing and cursive hands were commonly intermixed to a very late period. Gothic and cursive, he tells us, are found together in the common hands of the age of Elizabeth; what then? To have gained any real support to his cause he ought to have shown that the same admixture of hands prevailed in the middle of the seventeenth century.

III. Do the Notes and Emendations carry upon their face proofs of their genuineness?

The corrections and conjectural emendations which occur in the Devonshire folio are, so far as we have been made acquainted with them, of four descriptions:—

1. Typographical errors that are self-evident, and which could be corrected by the merest tyro in Shakespearian reading. ·

2. Typographical errors that require some critical acumen, or perhaps fancy, to amend. ·

3. Errors, the corrections of which have been made by other Commentators.

4. Errors that are corrected for the first time in the Devonshire folio.

Upon each of these divisions a few words are necessary. Unfortunately, however, this part of the case hardly admits of that complete examination which it demands, as Mr. Collier has failed to furnish us with all the necessary means for dealing with it. He has given to the world only those emendations which might seem to carry with them some air of probability; while three-fourths, at least, of their less fortunate brethren lie still unrevealed in the margins of this folio, there to remain until some future Editor shall deem them worth ushering into the light of day. But to proceed:—

1. The typographical errors that are self-evident, and which the merest tyro might correct, are such as *f*ight for fight, *f*aith for faith, *f*ail, for fail, &c., and reversing topsy-turvy letters, such as Mr. Collier describes.

2. Typographical errors that require some critical acumen or fancy to amend; such as " When *it* was out—let me not " live quoth he;" which is amended by Mr. Staunton thus, "When *wit* was out—let me not live quoth he."

It may be remarked, that corrections of this kind may be arrived at by three different processes:—(1.) By writing the suspected word in the hand of the 16th century, or by imitating the writing of Shakespeare, as far as possible, from the little that is known of it, and seeing how it would look in that writing; thus *law* which might be read either 'haste' or 'halter,' especially if it were carelessly written, or where the long *s* has been used by mistake for *f*, and *vice versâ*. (2.) By writing down the consonants or principal letters* of the doubted word, and guessing what the word ought to be, for at that period words were abbreviated by the omission of many of the vowels, as in *prnz*, which, being extended, might be read 'prinzie' or 'princely.' (3). By pronouncing the line or phrase rapidly, and catching the sense by the sound, as " I should not have thought it," which, when rapidly and not clearly pronounced, would sound like " I should not *of* thought it." " 'Tis not alone my inky cloak, good mother," which was misprinted in the edition of 1611, evidently from faulty pronunciation, " 'Tis not alone my incky cloake *could smother.*" Again, there are several instances where one word is mistaken for another by being pronounced more broadly, or slenderly, than usual, as in *wonder* and *wander*—*botcher* and *butcher*—*better* and *bitter*—*pin* and *pen*.

There is no doubt that a person resorting to any of these methods would frequently be able to correct corrupt readings, or at any rate produce clever suggestions. This seems to have been the mode adopted by the "Old Corrector;" and if he had confined himself to the exposure of such errors as he had by such means discovered, he would have been entitled to much praise for his ingenuity. But where he has allowed his unrestrained fancy or his ignorance to prevail, he has committed the most egregious blunders and absurdities.

---

* Shorthand may possibly have been employed in writing down from the mouths of the players those plays which were surreptitiously printed. Mr. Collier cites a passage from Heywood ("Life of Shakespeare," p. 142) in reference to the errors in plays thus procured and hastily printed, which proves that it was employed on some occasions :

" that some by stenography drew
The plot, put it in print scarce one word true."

But it is not at all probable that the manuscript which was supplied by the author or editor to the printer was ever in shorthand. It was doubtless occasionally written with the contractions in common use; as ꝓ for *pro*, ꝑ for *per*, *par*, *por*, ꝷ for *ter* or *tre*, ꝑ for *pre*, tⷫ for *tis* or *tes*, wᵗ for *what*, wᵗʰ for *with*, yᵗ for *that*, yᵉ for *the*, etc, and the compositors in extending such words frequently made mistakes.

On a rough calculation from the data furnished by Mr. Collier, the number of alterations in the Devonshire folio amounts to about 12,000, though he himself says near 20,000, which of course must include palpable mis-spellings and instances of incorrect punctuation. Taking the German Professor, Mommsem, for our authority, through the medium of the *Edinburgh Review*, there are 52 instances in which the initial letter of a word is altered, 7 in which it is added, 11 in which it is erased, 34 of initial double consonants altered, 95 of initials altered, together with other letters, 266 (if we count rightly) of final letters variously altered, and a proportional number of changes in letters between the first and the last. Mr. Collier has published about 2,700 of these alterations, leaving all others that occur in the folio unnoticed. Of the 2,700 so noticed, about 270 have been made by Malone, Theobald, Johnson, and others; the remainder being, almost entirely, worthless as blunders, or mere corrections of typographical errors. Judging from those which Mr. Collier has thus published, we are able to form some opinion of the value of those which he has declined to publish.

3. Errors, the corrections of which have been made by other Commentators.

A few of these, which have been taken at random from the various plays, will show to what extent his pilferings have been carried on by the " Old Corrector :"—

MEASURE FOR MEASURE.

Old or received text.	*" Old Corrector's" text.**
	ACT I. Sc. 5.
Sir, make me not your story.	Sir, make me not your *scorn.—Davenant.*
	ACT II. Sc. 4.
Proclaim an en-shield beauty.	Proclaim an *inshell'd* beauty.—*Tyrwhitt.*
	ACT V. Sc. 1.
Make rash remonstrance.	Make rash *demonstrance.—Malone.*

---

* The alterations by the " Old Corrector " are printed in Italics: at the end of each line is given the name of the Commentator from whom the " Old Corrector " is supposed to have borrowed the alteration.

COMEDY OF ERRORS.

Old or received text.   *" Old Corrector's" text.*

ACT V. Sc. 1.

The place of depth, and sorrie execution.   The place of *death* (¹) and *solemn* execution.—(¹) *Rowe.*

MIDSUMMER NIGHT'S DREAM.

ACT V. Sc. 1.

A lion fell, nor else no lion's dam.   A *lion's* fell, nor else no lion's dam.—*Baron Field.*

AS YOU LIKE IT.

ACT I. Sc. 1.

Bequeathed me by will.   *He* bequeathed me by will.—*Blackstone.*

ACT I. Sc. 3.

Some of it for my child's father.   Some of it for my *father's child.*—*Rowe.*

LOVE'S LABOUR LOST.

ACT I. Sc. 1.

A dangerous law against gentility.   A dangerous law against *garrulity.*—*Warburton* and *Theobald.*

ACT III. Sc. 1.

By my penne of observation.   By my *paine* of observation.—*Theobald.*

TAMING OF THE SHREW.

ACT I. Sc. 1.

Or so devote to Aristotle's checks.   Or so devote to Aristotle's *Ethics.*—*Blackstone.*

ACT I. Sc. 2.

My mind presumes, for his own good and yours.   My mind presumes, for his own good and *ours.**—*Theobald.*

ACT V. Sc. 2.

Hath cost me five hundred crowns since supper-time.   Cost me *one* hundred crowns since supper-time.—*Pope.*

MERRY WIVES OF WINDSOR.

ACT I. Sc. 3.

She carves, she gives the leer of invitation.   She *craves,* she gives the leer of invitation.—*Zach. Jackson.*

---

* This is omitted in the edition of the *Notes, Emendations,* etc. of 1856.

ALL'S WELL THAT ENDS WELL.

Old or received text.   *" Old Corrector's" text.*

Act II. Sc. 1.

Where hope is coldest and despair most shifts.

Where hope is coldest and despair most *fits.—Theobald.*

Act II. Sc. 3.

My honour's at the stake, which to defeat.

My honour's at the stake, which to *defend.—Theobald.*

Act II. Sc. 3.

To the dark house and the detected wife.

To the dark house and the *detested* wife.—*Rowe.*

Act III. Sc. 2.

Fly with false aim; move the still-peering air.

Fly with false aim; *wound* the still-*piecing* (¹) air.—(¹) *Malone.*

Act IV. Sc. 2.

I see that men make ropes in such a scarre.

I see that men make *hopes* in such a *suit.—Rowe.*

Act IV. Sc. 4.

And time revives us.

And time *reviles* us.—*Stevens.*

Act IV. Sc. 5.

Faith, Sir, a' has an English maine.

Faith, Sir, a' has an English *name.—Rowe.*

Act IV. Sc. 5.

And, indeed, he has no pace.

And, indeed, he has no *place.— Tyrwhitt.*

Act V. Sc. 3.

Done i' the blade of youth.

Done i' the *blaze* of youth.—*Theobald.*

Act V. Sc. 3.

Her insuit coming, with her modern grace.

Her *infinit cunning,* with her modern grace.—*Sidney Walker.*

TWELFTH NIGHT.

Act I. Sc. 1.

O! it came o'er my ear like the sweet sound.

O! it came o'er my ear like the sweet *south.—Pope.*

Old or received text.   " *Old Corrector's* " *text.*

ACT II. Sc. 5.

And with what wing the stallion checks at it.

And with what wing the *falcon** checks at it.

ACT IV. Sc. 1.

Adieu, goodman divel.

Adieu, goodman *drivel.—Farmer* and *Stevens.*

KING JOHN.

ACT II. Sc. 1.

His own determin'd aid.

His own determin'd *aim.—Mason.*

ACT III. Sc. 2.

Some airy devil hovers in the sky.

Some *fiery* devil hovers in the sky.—*Warburton.*

ACT V. Sc. 4.

Unthread the rude eye of rebellion.

Untread the *road-way* of rebellion.—*Theobald.*

FIRST PART OF HENRY IV.

ACT I. Sc. 1.

A conquest for a prince to boast of.

Faith 'tis a conquest for a prince to boast of.—*Pope.*

ACT I. Sc. 3.

Shall we buy treason, and indent with fears?

Shall we buy treason, and indent with *foes?*—*Hanmer.*

ACT I. Sc. 3.

I'll steal to Gloudower, and loo Mortimer.

I'll steal to Glendower, and *lord* Mortimer.—*All Editions* for upwards of a century.

ACT V. Sc. 2.

Supposition all our lives.

Suspicion all our lives.—*Pope.*

SECOND PART OF HENRY IV.

ACT I. Sc. 1.

The raggod'st hour.

The *rugged'st* hour.—*Theobald.*

ACT IV. Sc. 1.

Turning your books to graves.

Turning your books to *glaives.—Warburton.* (Stevens suggested *greaves.*)

---

* This alteration is one of the emendations pointed out by the *Edinburgh* Reviewer as a proof of the authenticity of the " Old Corrector." Now the word *stannyel* for *stallion* was happily suggested by Hanmer; and the Old Corrector for *stannyel* substitutes *falcon,* " which means nearly the same thing."

Old or received text.   *" Old Corrector's" text.*

HENRY V.

Act II. Sc. 1.

There shall be smiles.	There shall be *smites.—Farmer.*

Act II. Sc. 4.

Whiles that his mountain sire on mountain standing.	Whiles that his *mighty* sire on mountain standing.—*Tollet.*

Act III. Sc. 3.

Desire the locks.	*Defile* the locks.—*Pope.*

FIRST PART OF HENRY VI.

Act II. Sc. 4.

I scorn thee and thy fashion.	I scorn thee and thy *faction.—Theobald.*

Act III. Sc. 3.

On her lowly babe.	On her *lovely* babe.—*Warburton.*

Act V. Sc. 4.

The hollow passage of my poison'd voice.	The hollow passage of my *prison'd* voice.—*Pope.*

SECOND PART OF HENRY VI.

Act I. Sc. 3.

She'll gallop far enough.	She'll gallop *fast* enough.—*Pope.*

Act III. Sc. 2.

And to drain upon his face.	And to *rain* upon his face.—*Stevens.*

Act IV. Sc. 1.

The lives of those which we have lost in fight.	*Can* lives of those which we have lost in fight.—*Stevens.*

Act V. Sc. 3.

And all brush of time.	And all *bruise* of time.—*Warburton.*

THIRD PART OF HENRY VI.

Act I. Sc. 1.

Hear but one word.	Hear *me* but one word.—3d Folio, *Mason; Singer,* 1826.

Act II. Sc. 2.

And this soft courage.	And this soft *carriage.—Mason.*

Act V. Sc. 6.

To wit, an indigested deformed lump.	To wit, an *indigest* deformed lump.—*Malone*

RICHARD III.

| *Old or received text.* | " *Old Corrector's*" *text.* |

Act V. Sc. 3.

| To desperate adventures. | To desperate *ventures.—Stevens.* |

Act V. Sc. 3.

| They would restrain the one, distain the other. | They would *distrain* the one, distain the other.—*Warburton.* |

HENRY VIII.

Act I. Sc. 2.

| There is no primer baseness. | There is no primer *business.—Warburton.* |

Act I. Sc. 2.

| Whom after, under the commission's seal. | Whom after, under the *confession's* seal.—*Theobald.* |

Act I. Sc. 2.

| Things that are known alike. | Things that are known, *belike.—Theobald.* |

Act II. Sc. 3.

| I shall not fail t'approve the fair conceit. | I shall not fail *t'improve* the fair conceit.—*Knight.* |

Act V. Sc. 1.

| The good I stand on is my truth and honesty. | The *ground* I stand on is my truth and honesty.—*Johnson.* |

Act. V. Sc. 2.

| In our own natures frail and capable. | In our own natures frail and *culpable.—Theobald; Mason.* |

TROILUS AND CRESSIDA.

Act I. Sc. 1.

| So traitor, then she comes! | So traitor, *when* she comes!—*Rowe.* |

Act I. Sc. 1.

| As when the sun doth light a scorn. | As when the sun doth light a *storm.—Rowe.* |

Act I. Sc. 2.

| Achievement is command. | *Achiev'd men*[1] *still*[2] command.—[1]*Harness*; [2] *Collier's own emendation in a previous edition of Shakespeare.* |

Act. I. Sc. 3.

| Retires to chiding fortune. | *Replies* to chiding fortune.—*Hanmer.* |

Act II. Sc. 3.

| His pettish lines, his ebbs, his flows. | His pettish *lunes*, his ebbs, his flows.—*Hanmer.* |

Act III. Sc. 3.

| Keeps place with thought. | Keeps *pace* with thought.—*Hanmer.* |

CORIOLANUS.

Old or received text.	*" Old Corrector's" text.*

Act II. Sc. 1.

His soaring insolence shall teach the people.	His soaring insolence shall *touch* the people. —*Knight*.

Act II. Sc. 3.

See Singer's remark in "The text of Shakespeare Vindicated," *p.* 216, about the "Old Corrector" and Pope's line respecting Censorinus.

Act IV. Sc. 3.

But your favour is well appear'd by your tongue.	But your favour is well *approv'd* by your tongue.—*Stevens*.

Act IV. Sc. 4.

My birth place have I.	My birth place *hate* I.—*Stevens*.

ROMEO AND JULIET.

Act II. Sc. 2.

Lady, by yonder moon I vow.	Lady, by yonder *blessed* (¹) moon I *swear* (²). (¹) wanting only in the 1st Folio. (²) in the 4to. of 1597.

Act III. Sc. 5.

Tis but the pale reflex of Cynthia's brow.	'Tis but the pale reflex of Cynthia's *bow*.— *Singer*.

TIMON OF ATHENS.

Act I. Sc. 1.

Our poesy is a gown which uses.	Our poesy is a *gum* which *issues*.—*Pope*.

Act IV. Sc. 3.

It is the pastor lords the brother's sides.	It is the *pasture lards* the *rother's* sides.— *Singer*.

Act V. Sc. 2.

To stop affliction, let him take his haste.	To stop affliction, let him take his *halter*.*

---

* This example does not properly come under this head, but we have drawn attention to it because the *Edinburgh* Reviewer selects this alteration as proof of the genuineness of the emendations of the "Old Corrector," and remarks that "let *him take his haste*" is sheer nonsense, and yet it is so near sense that every Editor has passed it by without remark, as not worth touching.   The Corrector reads it "take his halter," and the Reviewer asks, "Why should a forger have gone out of his way to meddle with a text which no man had disturbed before?"   It is not necessary to point out the illogical inference drawn by the Reviewer, but the error, it should be remarked, does not lie in *haste* but in *take*. "Let him *make* his haste" is very good sense; but the "Old Corrector," not understanding the passage, thought the error was in *haste*, and

brought back the word to the writing of the sixteenth century; thus, *ℓασℓ*, which he thought would read either "halter" or "haste;" and then "boldly" (we use the Reviewer's own word) amends the text, and substitutes *halter* for *haste*.

Old or received text.   *" Old Corrector's" text.*

ACT V. Sc. 4.

Some beast read this; there does not live a man.

Some beast *rear'd* this; there does not live a man. — *Warburton.* See Staunton's restoration of this passage.

MACBETH.
ACT I. Sc. 4.

The swiftest { *wine* (1632) } { wing (1623) } of recompense is slow.

The swiftest *wind* of recompence is slow. —*Pope.*

Here are upwards of 70 emendations taken from 23 plays at hazard, in which the " Old Corrector " has anticipated the conjectures of Tyrwhitt, Rowe, Baron Field, Blackstone, Davenant, Knight, Singer, Theobald, Malone, Stevens, Sidney Walker, Pope, Hanmer, Jackson, Capell, Farmer, Mason, Warburton, Tollet, Johnson, and even Mr. Collier himself!

Upon the value of these emendations there is no necessity for comment * (beyond observing that many of the rejected readings of Malone and Hanmer have been adopted by the annotator of the Devonshire folio), because a question of far more importance to the present inquiry will occur to the reader. How came the " Old Corrector " to anticipate the conjectures of minds so various as these? Asmodeus, in Le Sage's story, sees, though certainly through brick walls, the deeds of existing men; but the " Old Corrector " performs a feat far more astonishing—he sees at a glance, and in embryo, all these, both probable and improbable, conjectures, which shall enter the fertile brains of Shakespearian critics and correctors, a century or more before those brains are yet in existence.

It might be said, and it cannot be denied, that, amid the thousands of suggestions made by Shakespearian critics of the last century and a half for amendment of the text, the probabilities are, in many instances, owing to a happy surmise, the correct reading would be restored,—such readings, in fact, as might have been within the personal knowledge of a scholar living in 1652; but if there are many instances in which the Old Corrector agrees with the suggesters of these happy emendations, the instances unfortunately are tenfold more numerous where he agrees with

---

* Perhaps the best test of the value of these emendations is the number of them which have been adopted by the last two Editors of Shakespeare, Messrs. Dyce and Staunton.

none of them, and where his alterations are not tenable for a moment. The only conclusion, then, that we can arrive at is, that for nearly all his emendations of the slightest value, this "Old Corrector" has been indebted, not to his personal acquaintance with the early actors of Shakespeare's plays, but to the whole body of Shakespearian critics since the time of Queen Anne; and that for the rest of his corrections, which from their utter worthlessness are self-condemned, he has been indebted, not to the early actors of Shakespeare's plays, but, as already suggested, to his own misdirected fancy. Mr. Collier (*" Notes and Emendations,"* p. xxi.,) asks " was he (the " Old Corrector ") indebted to his own sagacity and ingenuity, and did he merely guess at arbitrary emendations ? I am inclined to think that the last must have been the fact as regards some of the changes." With this opinion we readily concur ; only instead of *some changes,* we should suggest *most of the changes.*

4. Errors that are corrected for the first time in the Devonshire Folio.

The number of these emendations, as printed by Mr. Collier in his last Edition of them, amounts as already mentioned to about 2,400, which the *Edinburgh* Reviewer states is not one-fourth of all these readings. In "Hamlet" there are 463 MS. alterations in the Devonshire folio ; though Mr. Collier has noticed only 126 of them. The whole of them may be seen, however, in Mr. Hamilton's *"Inquiry, &c."* pp. 34–54. Now of some 2,000 guesses, it would be strange indeed if some few were not to the purpose. The dullest commentator that ever lived must have had a surprising faculty for perverseness if he could not sometimes blunder into the right reading, after so many years' practice as this unknown commentator must have enjoyed, and such continuous toil.

Dr. Delius, the well-known German Shakespearian critic, says Mr. R. Grant White,[*] after a careful consideration and examination of the Notes and Emendations printed by Mr. Collier, admits only 17 new readings as corrections worthy of adoption. Mr. Grant White likewise informs us, from the data supplied to him by Mr. Collier's *"Notes and Emendations,"* that the "Old Corrector" has made

---

[*] *Shakespeare's Scholar* (1854), p. 75.

thirteen hundred and three modifications of the text of the second folio. Of these thirteen hundred and three, at least two hundred and forty-nine are old; that is, either restorations of the text of the original folio, adoptions of readings from the old quartos, or identical with the conjectural emendations of editors and commentators during the last hundred and fifty years. Of these 249 old readings, 29 have long ago been rejected by common consent, as unworthy of the least attention ; 47 have been rejected from the text, but are allowed to have a certain plausibility ; and 173 are found in the received text.* Mr. White further states that Mr. Collier's emendations from the Devonshire folio contain 1,013 inadmissible alterations ; a total which would have been wonderfully increased had he counted the numbers in the folio itself. This, however, is no fault on the part of Mr. White ; he could only take his data from Mr. Collier's publications.

But what would twenty, or thirty, or even fifty, ingenious guesses be worth in determining the question of the authenticity of the " Old Corrector's " copy, if the remainder exhibited absurdities and misapprehensions of Shakespeare's meaning, as well as tawdry sentiments unworthy of the pen of Shakespeare's humbler contemporaries even ?

To make this plain, it will be necessary to place before the reader some of the emendations which Mr. Collier. has printed, in which it is clear that the " Old Corrector " has exhibited his utter incapacity to appreciate the poetic genius of the man whose works he undertook to amend, and that he must have gone into the highways and byeways to collect his materials, taking them indiscriminately as he found them. He cared not for quality; quantity was evidently his great object.

In addition to the many other liberties which the " Old Corrector " has taken with Shakespeare's works, he has presumed to add entire lines, and to alter the ends of others over and over again for the mere purpose of supplying a tag or rhyme, in the worst possible taste, and wholly destroying the sense of the passage which he professes to improve. These

---

* *Shakespeare's Scholar* (1854), p. 67.

are neither amendments nor corrections of existing errors; they supply no deficiency, but are mere useless additions. In fact, he has done that which was never intended to be done; he has washed pure gold with a lackering of brass.

It can hardly be denied, we should think, that a man's ear must have been greatly corrupted by dabbling in doggrel imitations of the ballad literature of the sixteenth and seventeenth centuries before he could venture to insert such lines* as these, for no apparent purpose beyond the gratification of a morbid taste for jingling rhymes :—

> " Inspire me that I may this treason finde,
> My lord, looke heere, looke heere Lavinia."
>
> *Altered to*
>
> " Inspire me that *this treason finde I may*,
> My lord, looke heere, looke heere Lavinia."

> " And madam, if my uncle Marcus goe,
> I will most willingly attend your ladyship."
>
> *Altered to*
>
> " And madam, if my uncle Marcus goe,
> I will most willingly attend *you so.*"

> " May run into that sinke, and soaking in,
> Drowne the lamenting foole in sea-salt-teares."
>
> *Altered to*
>
> " May run into that sinke, and soaking in,
> Drowne the lamenting foole *in sea-salt-brine.*"

> " No funerall Rite, nor man in mournfull weeds;
> No mournfull Bell shall ring her Buriall."
>
> *Altered to*
>
> " No funerall Rite, nor man in mournfull *pall* ;
> No mournfull Bell shall ring her Buriall."

> " For two and twenty sonnes I never wept,
> Because they died in honours lofty bed."
>
> *Altered to*
>
> " For two and twenty sonnes I never wept,
> Because in honours lofty bed they *slept.*"

> " And keep eternall spring-time on thy face,
> So thou refuse to drinke my deare sonnes blood."
>
> *Altered to*
>
> " And keep eternall spring-time in the *flood*,
> So thou refuse to drinke my deare sonnes blood."

---

* The Devonshire folio abounds in alterations of this description. With the exception of two (the last quoted in the next page), the instances here given have not been inserted by Mr. Collier in any of his editions. Nothing would so well show the utter worthlessness of these alterations as by printing all those which Mr. Collier has omitted.

> "Oh, be to me, though thy hard heart say no,
> Nothing so kind, but something pittiful."

Altered to

> "Oh, be to me, though thy hard heart say no,
> Nothiug so kiud, but *still some pity show.*"*

> "That hath expres't himselfe in all his deeds,
> A Father and a friend to thee and Rome."

Altered to

> "That hath expres't himselfe *abroad at home,*
> A Father and a friend to thee and Rome."

> *Queen.*—"I see no reason, why a king of yeares
> Should be to be protected like a child;
> God and King Henry governe England's Realme:
> Give up your staffe, Sir, and the King his Realme.
> *Glost.*—My staffe? Here, noble Henry, is my staffe,
> As willingly doe I the same resigne."

Altered to

> *Queen.*—"I see no reason, why a king of yeeres
> Should be to be protected like a child; *by peeres,*
> God and King Henry governe England's *helm,*
> Give up your staffe, Sir, and the King his Realme.
> *Glost.*—My staffe? Here, noble Henry, is my staffe,
> *To think I fain would keep it makes me laugh,*
> As willingly doe I the same resigne."

> "While I remaiue behind to tell a tale,
> That shall hereafter turne the hearers pale."†

> "Fight for your King, your Country, and your Lives;
> And so farewell, for I must hence again."

Altered to

> "Fight for your King, your Country, and your Lives:
> And so farewell: *rebellion never thrives.*"‡

Instances in which the "Old Corrector" has entirely misunderstood the sense:—

In "As You Like It," Act IV. Sc. 1.:

> *Orland.*—"Who could be out, being before his beloved mistress?
> *Rosal.*—Marry, that should you, if I were your mistress, or I should think my honesty ranker than my wit."

Rosalind's speech has been altered by the "Old Corrector" thus—

> "Marry, that should you, if I were your mistress, or I should *thank* my honesty *rather* than my wit."

What Shakespeare meant is clearly expressed. The "Old Corrector" by his amendment makes it sheer nonsense. For what should Rosalind thank her honesty?

---

* So altered, but afterwards struck out.
† These two lines are additions; but they are not published by Mr. Collier.
‡ The reader will remember the verse from which this "tag" was evidently derived:—

> "Treason can never prosper—for this reason:
> That if it prospers, none dare call it treason."

In "Henry the Fifth," Act II. Sc. 3., the Hostess, describing the death of Falstaff, says—

"'A parted eve'n just between twelve and one, e'en at the turning o' the tide; for after I saw him fumble with the sheets, and play with flowers, and smile upon his finger's ends, I knew there was but one way ; *for his nose was as sharp as a pen,*[*] *and 'a babbled*[†] *of green fields.*"

But the " Old Corrector " gives the passage in italics, thus—

" For his nose was as sharp as a pen *on a table of green frieze.*"

There is something exquisitely touching, as well as truthful, in Shakespeare's description of the dying old man, whose thoughts reverted to the innocence of his childhood, and to its "green fields;" and it is almost lamentable to think how the passage has thus been misunderstood and vulgarized by the " Old Corrector," who must have sadly taxed his ingenuity for the purpose of distorting the poet's meaning.

In "Henry the Fifth," Act IV. Sc. 1., Henry speaks of—

" ·   ·   ·   ·   the wretched slave,
Who, with a body fill'd, and vacant mind,
Gets him to rest, cramm'd with distressful bread."

The " Old Corrector " amends the third line thus—

" Gets him to rest, cramm'd with *distasteful* bread."

Thus robbing the figure of its poetical drapery, and dressing it in a patchwork robe.   Shakespeare's image is touching and beautiful.   We can picture the poor slave eating the bread of sorrow—distressful to his spirit—not as the "Old Corrector" suggests, distasteful to his stomach.

In " Cymbeline," Act III. Sc. 2., Imogen, eager to meet Posthumus, calls for horses, and when Pisanio submits that they can go no farther than twenty miles a day, she exclaims—

" ·   ·   ·   ·   I have heard of riding-wagers,
Where horses have been nimbler than the sands
That run 'i the clock's behalf."

This simile is perfect—meaning that the horses are nimbler than the sands that run in the hour-glass—substituted for a clock.   The " Old Corrector " makes Imogen speak thus—

" ·   ·   ·   ·   Nimbler than the sands,
That run 'i the clocks, *by half.*"

---

* This is probably a misprint for *pin.*
† In the folio editions of Shakespeare, the above final words are incorrectly printed, " and *a table* of green fields," which Theobald most happily restored as given above.

An emendation that is ridiculous. In addition to misapprehending Shakespeare, the "Old Corrector" has made an egregious blunder, by making the sands a portion of the works of a clock; the horses are nimbler by half than the sands that run in a clock ! !

In "The Tempest," Act I. Sc. 2., Prospero says—

> "One,
> Who having, unto truth, by telling of it,
> Made such a sinner of his memory,
> To credit his own lie."

The text of this passage is certainly obscure; but the "Old Corrector" has made it no less so. He gives it thus :-

> "One,
> Who having *to untruth*, by telling of it,
> Made such a sinner of his memory,
> To credit his own lie."

There is something eminently absurd in the following alteration. In the Induction of "The Taming of the Shrew," Sc. 2. Christopher Sly says,—"If she say I am not fourteen pence on the score for sheer ale, score me up for the lyingest knave in Christendom."

The meaning is clear enough, and yet the "Old Corrector," out of sheer wantonness, one might almost think, alters the passage thus : "If she say I am not fourteen pence on the score for *Warwickshire* ale, score me up, etc." And Mr. Collier gives someequally baseless justification of the alteration ; whereas "*sheer*" here signifies nothing more or less than *pure* or *unmixed* (equivalent to the Latin *merus*), an expression still in common use. Johnson even selects his example of the use of this word from the drunken Tinker's speech ; but the "Old Corrector," perhaps, wished to improve on what Malone had suggested on the subject, who thought that it meant *shearing* or reaping ale.

---

* We would, however, suggest the following reading—

> " One,
> Who *adding* unto truth by telling of it,
> Made such a sinner of his memory,
> To credit his own lie."

That is, he had exaggerated truth so often, that at last he believed his own exaggeration.

A few words are called for in reference to the numerous passages which are struck out in the Devonshire folio. The principal purpose of these mutilations seems to have been to shorten the Scenes, for they occur in the plays that were most frequently performed. Some few passages, however, may have been struck out because the audience did not understand them, and some, though not many, as Mr. Collier suggests, on account of their indecency. It has been asked, if these corrections are really forged, what motive could any modern forger have in eliminating a number of magnificent passages from the folio? Would he have ventured to incur the odium of such imprudence? So far, however, from there being any intrinsic value in this suggestion, the friends of the folio have far from mended their case by inviting attention to the fact; one in itself most strange and most unaccountable, on the supposition of the genuineness of the corrections in the folio.

There are throughout the book a number of the finest passages scored out, as is common in prompters' copies. (A copy of the same edition in fact is now lying open before us, in which some of the most poetical passages are similarly struck out.) It is assumed that these elisions in the Devonshire folio must have been made by the "Old Corrector," in conformity with some original from which he derived his emendations. Now the overwhelming probability seems to be, that the passages in question were *not* struck out by the person who wrote the Notes and Emendations, but were expunged at a much *earlier* period, and that solely for theatrical, and not critical, purposes; the ink in which the corrections are made being evidently different from that in which these deletions or elisions occur. This fact too seems the more clear, as these scored passages are accompanied by exactly the same sort of amended readings in the margin as the rest of the book. If they were scored out by the "Old Corrector" with the view of being omitted, how came they, equally with the unscored passages, to exhibit these various readings?

A word or two also on the punctuation and stage directions which have been added throughout the Devonshire volume; a point of some importance, although little attention seems to have been directed to it throughout this controversy. On this subject Mr. Collier writes :—" The changes in punctuation alone, always made with nicety and patience, must have required a long period, considering their number; the other alterations, sometimes most minute, extending even to turned letters and typographical trifles of that kind, from their very nature could not have been introduced with rapidity."

Now it is greatly to be doubted whether Mr. Collier, with all his experience in such matters, can show any other instance, in dramas of the first half of the seventeenth century, either manuscript or printed, where such minutiæ are to be found. Every one must know, who has given the slightest attention to the subject, that the punctuation introduced into this folio is not the punctuation of the seventeenth century, nor even of the eighteenth. It is too elaborate to be genuine. Indeed, it may be doubted whether an editor, in preparing an edition for press in the present century, could have been more exact. The volume has all the appearance in fact of having been actually punctuated for press;* and, singular to say, minute as this punctuation is, and savouring so strongly of the present century, it unquestionably was inserted in pencil before it was written in ink, as in many instances it underlies the ink.

In reference also to the stage directions,—they are much too abundant to be genuine. In fact, Mr. Collier has remarked that the written additions of this kind seem even more frequent and more explicit than might be thought necessary. It may be observed, that many of the stage directions prove that the corrections were not made at the time to which they professedly belong; for painted or moveable scenery (especially of such a character as trees into which a person might climb) was not in use

---

* No one, we feel persuaded, who has carefully examined the volume, can come to any other conclusion than that this folio was corrected with the full intention of printing it; why that intention was abandoned, it is not for us to surmise. In this respect, we perfectly agree with the writer in the *Edinburgh Review*, who states, that "not only are words and sentences altered, lines added, omitted, or transposed, but the orthography and punctuation are set right with the minutest and most fastidious care."

at that period.* When, therefore, we find in "Love's Labours Lost," Act IV. Sc. 3., where the original direction "*He stands aside*" is obliterated, and "*He gets him in a tree*" is written in its place in manuscript; when, too, Biron interposes some remark to himself, and it is added, "He is *in the tree*," and when upon his descending to detect his companions "*Come down*" is inscribed in the margin,— these alterations are more than suspicious; indeed, they are fatal to the antiquity of the directions. A similar remark applies also to the alteration in "Much Ado About Nothing," Act II. Sc. 3., where Benedick says "I will hide me in the arbour," the "Old Corrector" having added, "*Retires behind the trees.*" In some instances the printed stage directions have been obliterated; in others, again, the stage instructions of undoubtedly a succeeding century have been anticipated. No one knows better than Mr. Collier that there is a dearth of them in all early printed dramas, and he admits that in the old printed copies there is but one note of *aside* in the whole of Shakespeare's thirty-six plays. Surely, then, these facts must afford some ground at least for the suspicion that these additions were not inserted until long after the time at which the emendations are alleged to have been made.

So far, too, from it being probable that any person at all conversant with the usages of the stage would commit to paper minutiæ of this description, it is the fact that many of the stage directions are traditional, and handed down

---

* Painted scenery was not in use at public theatres until after the Restoration, though it was undoubtedly introduced into Masques at Court and a few private exhibitions at an earlier period. The advocates for the genuineness of the Notes and Emendations in the Devonshire folio may possibly contend that these stage-directions were inserted after the Restoration. This position, however, is not tenable, as the writing in which they occur is a hand professedly of earlier date. Indeed, Mr. Collier himself evidently admits that they are of earlier date, for he says that "these stage-directions are of the highest importance in illustrating the wonderful judgment and skill of Shakespeare in conducting the business of the scenes;"—implying that they must have come immediately from Shakespeare himself. Also, in his affidavit of the 8th January 1856, he says that he has not inserted a single word, stop, sign, note, correction, alteration, or emendation, which is not a faithful copy of the original manuscript, and which he believes *to have been written* not *long after the publication of the folio copy of the year* 1632. The reader who is interested in this portion of the history of our Drama may consult "An Historical Account of the English Stage," vol. iii., pp. 79–109 in the *Variorum* edition of Shakespeare, 1813; as also the *Historia Histrionica* by Wright, published in 1699; and Collier's *Annals of the Stage*, vol. iii., p. 365, *et seq.*

from actor to actor; consequently, there would be no need either to print or to write them for the information of persons who would as a matter of course learn their bye-play from the oral communications of their stage-managers, who, in their turn, learned them in a similar manner from their predecessors belonging to the theatre.

Another suspicious circumstance in connexion with these emendations is the liberty taken by the " Old Corrector " in modernizing words. He has not stopped, as the *Edinburgh* Reviewer remarks, at his own supposed day, but has absolutely brought his modernizings down to the present century.

At the close of this branch of the inquiry, it may be not irrelevant to remark that whatever else may have been accomplished by the researches of the non-believers in the Notes and Emendations of the Devonshire folio, this at least has been done :—they have been the means of bringing forward evidence utterly destructive of the authority of the " Old Corrector." Even the most ardent supporters of the " Old Corrector " must now hesitate before they accept his emendations as valid authority *per se* of any reading; and that, after all, is the more important branch of the question. Who the interpolator may have been is a matter of comparative indifference.

IV. What is the history of the folio in which these notes and emendations are found?

At the risk of seeming tedious, it will be necessary to recapitulate under this head many details with which most readers of these pages will in all probability be familiar. Viewed as a matter of feeling, the *Edinburgh* Reviewer is fully justified, no doubt, in his remark that the subject is a painful one to approach; but justice alike to the impugners of the Devonshire folio and to Mr. Collier himself demands that it should not be passed over in silence.

As already stated, from the very moment that Mr. Collier gave to the world a sample of the Notes and Emendations in his folio, grave doubts were entertained of their genuineness; and no long period elapsed before he was assailed on all sides by Shakespearian critics, who asserted that an attempt had been made upon their credulity, notwithstanding the statement given in his Preface relative to the volume. Having, however, been more directly attacked in an anonymous pamphlet, entitled " Literary Cookery," Mr. Collier thought it necessary to make an affidavit on the subject in the Court of Queen's Bench, in which he swore to the truth of the facts stated in his Preface, and made some further disclosures respecting the history of his obtaining possession of the volume in question.

As some new materials have been recently imported into this part of the case, which are at variance with Mr. Collier's statement, it will be necessary to give his own version of the story ;* which is as follows :—

" In the history of the volume to which I have been thus indebted, I can offer little that may serve to give it authenticity. It is very certain that the manuscript notes in its margins were made before it was subjected to all the ill-usage it experienced. When it first came into my hands, and indeed for some time afterwards, I imagined that the binding was the original rough calf in which many books of about the same date were clothed; but more recent examination has convinced me, that this was at least the second coat it had worn. It is, nevertheless, in a very shabby condition, quite consistent with the state of the interior, where, besides the loss of some leaves, as already mentioned, and the loosening of others, many stains of wine, beer, and other liquids are observable ; here and there holes have been burned in the paper, either by the falling of the lighted snuff of a candle, or by the ashes of tobacco. In several places it is torn and disfigured by blots and dirt, and every margin bears evidence to frequent and careless perusal. In short, to a choice collector, no book could well present a more forbidding appearance.

" I was tempted only by its cheapness to buy it, under the following circumstances :—In the spring of 1849 I happened to be in the shop of the late Mr. Rodd, of Great Newport Street, at the time when a package of books arrived from the country ; my impression is that they came from Bedfordshire ; but I am not at all certain upon

---

* *Notes and Emendations* (1852)—Introduction, p. v.

a point which I looked upon as a matter of no importance. He opened the parcel in my presence, as he had often done before in the course of my thirty or forty years' acquaintance with him; and, looking at the backs and title pages of several volumes, I saw that they were chiefly works of little interest to me. Two folios, however, attracted my attention; one of them gilt on the sides, and the other in rough calf. The first was an excellent copy of Florio's "New World of Words," 1611, with the name of Henry Osborn (whom I mistook at the moment for his celebrated namesake, Francis,) upon the first leaf; and the other a copy of the second folio of Shakespeare's Plays, much cropped, the covers old and greasy, and as I saw at a glance on opening them, imperfect at the beginning and end. Concluding hastily that the latter would complete another poor copy of the second folio, which I had bought of the same bookseller, and which I had for some years in my possession, and wanting the former for my use, I bought them both, the Florio for twelve, and the Shakespeare for thirty shillings."

Mr. Collier goes on to state, "As it turned out, I at first repented of my bargain as regarded the Shakespeare, because, when I took it home it appeared that two leaves which I wanted were unfit for my purpose, not merely by being too short, but damaged and defaced; thus disappointed I threw it by, and did not see it again until I made a selection of books I would take with me on quitting London. In the mean time, finding that I could not readily remedy the deficiencies in my other copy of the folio 1632, I had parted with it; and when I removed into the country with my family in the spring of 1850, in order that I might not be without some copy of the second folio, for the purpose of reference, I took with me that which is the foundation of the present work.

"It was while putting my books together for removal, that I first observed some marks in the margin of this folio; but it was subsequently placed upon an upper shelf, and I did not take it down until I had occasion to consult it."

"It then struck me that Thomas Perkins, whose name, with the addition "his book," was upon the cover, might be the old actor, who had performed in Marlowe's "Jew of

Malta," on its revival shortly before 1633. At this time
I fancied that the binding was of about that date, and that the
volume might have been his ; but in the first place I found
that his name was Richard Perkins, and in the next I
became satisfied that the rough calf was not the original
binding. Still, Thomas Perkins might have been a descen-
dant of Richard ; and this circumstance, and others, induced
me to examine the volume more particularly. I then
discovered, to my surprise, that there was hardly a page
which did not present, in a handwriting of the time, some
emendation in the pointing or in the text, while on most of
them they were frequent and on many numerous."

Further examination led to more important discoveries.—
" Of course I now submitted the folio to a most careful
scrutiny; and as it occupied a considerable time to complete the inspection, how much more must it have consumed
to make the alterations? The ink was of various shades,
differing sometimes on the same page, and I was once
disposed to think that two distinct hands had been employed
upon them. This notion I have since abandoned; and I
am now decidedly of opinion that the same writing prevails
from beginning to end, but that the amendments must
have been introduced from time to time, during perhaps
the course of several years. The changes in punctuation
alone, always made with nicety and patience, must have
required a long period, considering their number; the
other alterations, sometimes most minute, extending even to
turned letters, and typographical trifles of that kind, from
their very nature could not have been introduced with
rapidity, while many of the errata must have severely tasked
the industry of the Old Corrector."

Such is Mr. Collier's statement in the year 1852, when
he first printed some of these emendations in an 8vo.
volume, before any suspicions had been raised as to their
genuineness.

The statement thus put forth at leisure eight years ago,
when the circumstances were more recent in his memory,
was repeated by him in the following year, when he brought
out a second edition; but, with an extraordinary reticence
and inconceivable self-restraint, for which there is no
satisfactory or assignable motive, instead of publishing these

corrections at once, he dribbled them out piecemeal; first in the volume of 1852, "containing some, but not all the said MS. Emendations, &c. ;" then in a second edition of the volume, which was published in 1853; and next in a one-volume Shakespeare,* published also in 1853, where such of them were given as "did not seem to require distinct and separate mention among the *Notes and Emendations* recently published." A professedly Complete List appeared only in 1856, at the end of Mr. Collier's edition of Coleridge's *Seven Lectures on Shakespeare and Milton ;* and now it is in evidence that this professedly Complete List does not comprise one half of the manuscript emendations that exist in this folio; while, on the other hand, many that had appeared in the above-mentioned publications of 1852 and 1853, are not to be found in the List of 1856.†

Now such a mode of proceeding as this, really seems irreconcileable with the ordinary motives which actuate mankind; indeed, the writer in the *Edinburgh Review* himself, favourable as he is to Mr. Collier and the claims of the folio, cannot disguise his annoyance, when speaking of it.

"In possession of the mysterious volume," says the Reviewer, " Mr. Collier proceeded, however, to deal with it in so strangely inconsistent and inadequate a manner as to rouse, not unnaturally, the suspicions of his many ill-wishers. True to the instinct of his former literary career, always fumbling with the text of Shakespeare, advancing new conjectures and new discoveries by piecemeal, and never taking counsel of time and silence to ripen his own convictions, he first brought out, in 1853, his volume called ' Notes and Emendations from early MS. Corrections,' but which comprised a great deal of conjectural matter besides these corrections, and gave only fragments of the corrections themselves. Then followed his one volume edition of Shakespeare, professing to incorporate the corrections, but really incorporating only some of them, and without the slightest attempt to enable the reader to find out where the corrections are; respecting which, we are half inclined to echo the sentiments of the infuriated Mr. Grant White :—' With all

---

* *The Plays of Shakespeare;* the text regulated by the Old Copies, and by the recently discovered Folio of 1632, containing early MS. emendations.
† See Note, page 40.

respect due from me to a gentleman, who was a man when my father was a boy, I must say that the publication of that volume was a crime against the republic of 'letters.' And, lastly, to omit other intermediate fidgettings with the subject, he published in 1856 his 'Seven Lectures on Shakespeare and Milton' (a compilation from alleged original Notes, in which some hostile eyes have seen another forgery), and for some inscrutable reason, added, in an Appendix to this volume, what he terms 'A List of every Note and Emendation in Mr. Collier's copy of Shakespeare's works,' but which really contains, says Mr. Hamilton, not above half the emendations, we should have fancied, hardly a third or a fourth."

How, it may here be parenthetically inquired, can the writer of this article reconcile these statements of his own with his avowed belief in the alleged history of this unhappy folio since the year 1849?

Mr. Collier says, in his affidavit sworn in the Court of Queen's Bench, in 1856 :—

" And I say, that all the statements in the said preface and introduction, relative to the discovery, contents, and authenticity of the said folio copy, and the manuscript notes, corrections, alterations, and emendations thereof, are true; and that every note, correction, alteration, and emendation in each of the said two editions, and every word, figure, and sign therein purporting or professing to be a note, correction, alteration, or emendation of the text, is, to the best of my knowledge and belief, a true and accurate copy of the original manuscript in the said folio copy of 1632; and that I have not, in either of the said editions, to the best of my knowledge and belief, inserted a single word, stop, sign, note, correction, alteration, or emendation of the said original text of Shakespeare, which is not a faithful copy of the said original manuscript, and which I do not believe to have been written, as aforesaid, not long after the publication of the said folio copy of the year 1632."

According to Mr. Collier's reiterated statements,* *all* the emendations contained in the " Old Corrector" are

---

* Preface to *Coleridge's Lectures*, pp. 60, 73, and 79.

printed in his List of 1856, whereas it is now admitted that scarcely one-fourth is to be found therein; while again it is not a little singular that many of the emendations contained in the before-mentioned publications of 1853 are left out in the List of 1856.*

Again, in his *Reply* to Mr. Hamilton's letter, Mr. Collier refers to his affidavit sworn and filed in the Queen's Bench, January 8th, 1856; and he further states,--" I have shown and sworn that this very book was in the possession of a gentleman named Parry about half a century ago, given to him by a relation named George Gray."

On no point has Mr. Collier laboured more than to prove that the Devonshire folio belonged to Mr. Parry; yet he

---

* The reader is not required to accept this fact upon assertion only. He is referred to Mr. Collier's three versions; they are the evidence in the matter.

Two or three instances, however, may be subjoined of the omission of emendations in the " *Complete List* " of 1856, which had appeared in the earlier editions. At page 222 of the edition of 1853, Mr. Collier states, " The folio of 1632 misprints the following line :—

"Give sorrow leave a while to tutor me,"

by absurdly putting *return* for 'tutor.' This blunder is *set right by the Old Corrector;* but it seems as if he had previously substituted some other word, and had erased it. *Such may have been the case in several other places* where he himself blundered." These are Mr. Collier's words, italics and all, upon which Mr. Singer remarks :—

"This is hardly candid on the part of Mr. Collier, for who would not think that 'this blunder was set right' by the sagacity of the corrector; whereas it is only the reading of the first folio, where the word is *tuture*, and the misprint had been corrected in all editions! Do not the frequent *erasures* in this corrected volume excite any suspicion in Mr. Collier's mind that it has been extensively tampered with."

After Mr. Singer's allegation, in these terms, of Mr. Collier's want of candour, Mr. Collier has thought proper to leave out the emendation in his " *Complete List*" of 1856.

In 1853 Mr. Collier writes, " The Corrector has ' as *surely* as I live,' of the quarto of 1597, instead of 'as sure as I live,' which is the reading of some of the folios and some of the quartos." Mr. Singer points out this emendation as a remarkable coincidence with Mr. Collier's adoption of it from the quarto of 1597. After Mr. Singer's remark, Mr. Collier forbears to insert this emendation in his List of 1856.

Again, in reference to the line which appeared for the first time in the Devonshire folio :—

" To brook control without the use of anger,"—(*Coriolanus*, Act iii. Sc. 2.)

Mr. Collier has adopted the line in his edition of Shakespeare of 1858, but has changed the word *control* to *reproof*, with this remark, " This line is from the corrected folio of 1632, and is clearly wanted, since the sense is incomplete without it." Mr. Collier, however, makes no allusion to the fact that he had three times previously (in 1852, 1853, and 1856,) printed the line in the form given above.

appears (undoubtedly, in the first instance, and, according to Mr. Parry's statement, throughout the whole transaction,) to have neglected the means which above all others would have enabled him to obtain his desired end; viz., the exhibiting of the volume to Mr. Parry. Mr. Collier admits that he did not exhibit it to him until after his Preface to his edition of 1853 was finished, though he had talked to him about the volume more than once; while Mr. Parry, on the other hand, has publicly denied every particular that Mr. Collier has asserted; and his truthfulness and memory, it may be presumed, although Mr. Collier's senior by some years, are as much to be relied upon as Mr. Collier's. Mr. Parry can gain nothing by denying that the Devonshire folio ever was his property, while Mr. Collier would be no loser if he could prove it was.

In addition to this denial on the part of Mr. Parry, it now appears that, while searching among his books and papers, he has discovered the fly-leaf of his folio copy (which had come loose while it was in his possession), and it has been compared with the Devonshire folio. The result is, that it does not fit this copy at all, being a quarter of an inch too short, and a quarter of an inch too broad; a fact which goes far towards substantiating Mr. Parry's declaration, when he first saw the Devonshire folio at the British Museum, and from which he has never deviated, that the margins of his copy were wider than those of the (Devonshire) folio.

Mr. Collier, failing in his endeavour to prove that his folio had belonged to Mr. Parry, and feeling it necessary to adduce evidence that he bought the volume of Rodd in 1849, made application to Dr. Wellesley by letter, a copy of which surely ought to have been given, in addition to the Doctor's answer. That answer, which Mr. Collier kept to himself for six months before he thought proper to publish it, is as follows:—

"Woodmancote Rectory, Hurstpierpoint,
August 13th, 1859.

"Sir,

"Although I do not recollect the precise date, I remember some years ago being in the shop of Thomas Rodd on one occasion when a case of books from the country had just been opened. One of those books was an imperfect folio Shakespeare, with an abundance of manuscript notes in the

margins.   He observed to me that it was of little value to
collectors as a copy, and that the price was thirty shillings,
I should have taken it myself; but, as he stated that he had
put it by for another customer, I did not continue to examine
it; nor did I think any more about it, until I heard afterwards that it had been found to possess great literary
curiosity and value.   In all probability, Mr. Rodd named
you to me; but whether he or others did so, the affair
was generally spoken of at the time, and I never heard
it doubted that you had become the possessor of the
book.

"I am, Sir,

"Your faithful and obedient servant,

"H. WELLESLEY."

" To J. P. Collier, Esq."

What was *generally* spoken of?—that Mr. Collier had
purchased an imperfect folio of the second edition of Shakespeare, which (as he himself says) Mr. Rodd considered of
no value?   Was there anything remarkable in a man buying
such a book?   Even at this time that edition is by no means
unattainable, and even less so was it then.   But if the affair
was *generally* spoken of, how is it that Mr. Collier was wholly
ignorant of the reputation which he had thus gained?   How,
in fact, is this statement of Dr. Wellesley reconcileable with
Mr. Collier's assertion of his indifference for, and neglect of,
his new acquisition for a considerable period of time, a whole
year, at the very least?*   It seems altogether impossible to
bring these conflicting statements into anything like con-
sistency.

We do not at all impeach Dr. Wellesley's veracity, and
readily admit that he has stated his impression of the facts;
a statement quite reconcileable with the hypothesis that
Mr. Collier did purchase a folio Shakespeare of Mr. Rodd
in a very imperfect condition, scribbled over with marginal
annotations of no value, as such copies often are; but it
is our belief that the copy which Dr. Wellesley saw, and
which Rodd described to him as of *little value to collectors,*

---

* "It remained *long in my possession before* I became acquainted with its
great literary curiosity and value." (Collier's *Reply*, p. 10.) See the particulars
as to the intervening lapse of time, in pages 36, 37, *ante.*

was not the copy which Mr. Collier calls the "Perkins Folio."*

Mr. Rodd, we are told, asserted that the copy he sold for 30s. was of little value to collectors. Would he have asserted this of a folio of 1632, enriched with marginal notes and emendations, and those apparently in the hand-writing of that period? Certainly not, or he would have acted in a manner that no other dealer in old books in this kingdom would.

Mr. Rodd was in the habit of buying and disposing of MSS., and books with MS. emendations, to the British Museum; which would have given him, probably, many times as many pounds, and would have been eager to possess the volume. He, too, was at that time the London Agent for the Shakespearian Society's publications. If there was one subject which he thoroughly understood, and one in which he took a commendable pride, it was in the matter of Shakespearian literature and Shakespearian emendations; and his great sagacity in such matters, equally with his interest, would prompt him to examine, with more than usual attention, all the MS. notes and names in works of this description.

Mr. Collier states, that neither Mr. Rodd nor himself was aware of the existence of any manuscript notes in the volume which he bought for thirty shillings; if so, Mr. Rodd must have known nothing about the inside of the volume. On what grounds, then, did Mr. Rodd fix the price? He knew that the true value depended entirely on the condition of the volume. Is it at all likely then that he would have fixed the price and sold the book without having first examined it, to ascertain its precise condition? Mr. Rodd was not the man to have been guilty of such an unbusiness-like proceeding. Moreover, it has been already shown, from Dr. Wellesley's letter, that Mr. Rodd *had* examined the volume, and

---

* "It may not be necessary to say more on the present occasion than that the Perkins folio came out of a parcel of books from the country; that I was in Rodd's shop when the parcel arrived; that I bought it for thirty shillings (neither Rodd nor myself being aware of any manuscript notes in it)." *Reply,* pp. 7, 8.

pronounced it "of little value;" a thing that he certainly could never have said of the Devonshire folio, unless he had previously examined it, and had come to the conclusion that the emendations were worthless. In fact, the only inference that can fairly be drawn from Dr. Wellesley's letter is this, that if the volume he saw had been the Devonshire folio, Mr. Rodd's attention (supposing for a moment that it had not been previously given to it) would at that time, and from the very nature of Dr. Wellesley's inquiry, have infallibly been drawn to it; he would at once have seen that it was no ordinary volume, and would have lost no time in apprizing Mr. Collier of the lucky purchase which (to his own loss) he had made. Instead of which, Mr. Rodd, we are left to presume, let Mr. Collier take away his precious acquisition without one word more on the subject, to repose for at least twelve months on the shelves of one of the most indefatigable Shakespearian inquirers of the day, without being examined!

But Mr. Collier, we are told, purchased the volume in order to supply some missing leaves in a poor copy of that edition which he had already bought of the same bookseller. He would, therefore, naturally look into it to see whether or not it contained the leaves he wanted. On looking into it, could he possibly have failed to see that it was positively studded with marginal emendations thoughout?

How was it that he did not discover them at once? Did he by instinct open the volume at the very places where the pages he wanted ought to have been? And did he studiously avoid opening it anywhere else?

Let the reader take any copy of Shakespeare, the one even that he has in common use, and let him see whether he can hit, at two successive openings, on two given pages, in two plays, without making a search for them. Mr. Collier must either have done this, or he must have gone over the leaves to see if the volume contained those which he required; in doing the latter of which, it would seem to be wholly impossible that he could escape seeing the emendations which he himself tells us " were on most of the pages frequent, and on many numerous."

Taking all these points into consideration, it is impossible to avoid coming to the conclusion that Mr. Collier's account of the whole of this branch of the question is anything but satisfactory.   .

V. We proceed to the fifth division of this inquiry, viz., whether certain Letters and Papers relating to matters of Shakespearian interest, which Mr. Collier has printed or referred to, are genuine or not.

To begin with "The Players' Petition," a document at present in the State Paper Branch of the Public Record Office.—It is without date, but purports to be a Petition to the Lords of Queen Elizabeth's Council, from certain Players (eight of whom are therein named, one of them being "William Shakespeare,") praying their Lordships' permission that they may finish the reparations and alterations in their Theatre in the precinct of the Blackfriars, and that their performances there may not be interrupted. Mr. Collier calls it "a Counter Petition by the Lord Chamberlain's Players," and he was the first to direct public attention to it, by printing it in his *"Annals of the Stage"* (1831). He there announces his belief that it is not the original Petition, but merely a copy without the signatures.

Now, if the paper thus printed by Mr. Collier be only a copy of the Petition, it is at least a very unaccountable circumstance that the *copy* should have been preserved in the public archives, and the *original* not be found there as well.

We can quite understand why a fabricator (not aware that it was unusual for petitioners, during the reigns of Elizabeth and James I., to subscribe their names to Petitions) should prefer that a document fabricated by him should be considered as a *copy*, rather than as an *original*, seeing that the former could be much more easily manufactured than the other. He may have thought that in a document of this nature, if professing to be an original, it would be necessary to forge the signatures of eight persons,—a puzzling and awkward process; for though he might know how to imitate the signatures of some, yet he might not be acquainted with the signatures of all, and the failure of one would be the condemnation of the whole.

Mr. Collier, however, in one instance, says, "This remarkable paper has, perhaps, never seen the light, from the moment it was first presented, until it was recently discovered." Here he would seem to treat the document as an *original*, though in another place he has distinctly called it a *copy*. If it is not a contemporary copy,* the original would surely have been among the State Papers when the copy was made; and if it is a contemporary copy, why was it made? Surely not for the purpose of being preserved as a State Paper in lieu of the original.

Mr. Lemon, of the State Paper Branch Record Office, might possibly be able to throw some light on the subject; at any rate, as he is pretty confident of the fact of his father bringing the document in question under the notice of Mr. Collier, he ought to be able to say, with something like an equal degree of confidence, whether it was the *original* or the *copy* that his father placed before Mr. Collier, or both. And here, even at the risk of giving pain to Mr. Lemon, we must say, that in penning his hasty letter to the *Athenæum* (No. 1686), he has cast at least a shadow of a reproach upon his father's memory, by implying that he produced this " Petition " to Mr. Collier as a genuine document. If Mr. Lemon, Senior, really did produce this Petition, and pronounce it genuine, his judgment was marvellously at fault: but of the two alternatives, we should be inclined rather to doubt the accuracy of the son's memory than the father's skill as a palæographer; for we say, and say advisedly, that any one who could pronounce the "Players' Petition" to be genuine, would be totally unfit to hold the office that Mr. Lemon, Senior, held.

But supposing for a moment that the " Players' Petition ' was a genuine document, and that the fact of its existence

---

* Although slightly anticipating what will be more fully discussed hereafter, this most curious coincidence here calls for some notice, that several of the spurious documents that have been noticed or printed by Mr. Collier are termed by him *copies*, instead of originals; viz., The Players' Petition; The Memorial attached to the Players' Petition; The Certificate from the Players of the Blackfriars Theatre to the Privy Council in 1859; The Letter signed H. S., and other papers in which Shakespeare's name occurs. Is it not "strange, passing strange," that copies of all these papers should have been religiously preserved, the *originals* being nowhere to be found?

had been discovered by Mr. Lemon, his first duty, on such discovery, would be to communicate the fact to Mr. Hobhouse, the head of his office, and to make an entry of the purport of the document in the official Repertory. There is no evidence that he did either; on the contrary, the Petition was never heard of by the public until Mr. Collier printed it in 1831. Viewing the matter, too, as one of feeling, and laying aside all considerations of duty, if Mr. Lemon, Senior, had indeed discovered this precious document, and been convinced of its genuineness, no reasonable doubt can be entertained that he would have been too eager to announce the fact to the public, and that the whole of literary England would have rung with the intelligence of his good fortune. He, of all men, was not the person to conceal it from the chief of his office, from his colleagues, from his personal friends, and from the whole body of Shakespearian scholars. He was much too alive to the pleasure of congratulation to have kept such a discovery secret for a period of four years (1825 to 1829), and then to have communicated it to Mr. Collier, at that time an unknown individual, and recently introduced to him by a mere acquaintance. Such, however, is Mr. Collier's statement. But how comes it that he never thought of this before? One would certainly suppose that Mr. Collier would have made some mention (as he has done in instances where Mr. Lemon* had introduced a document to his notice) of Mr. Lemon's kindness in placing a document of such surpassing interest as this before him; but, on the contrary, not the slightest allusion is there made to him in connexion with the "Players' Petition," although Mr. Collier states that it had been very recently discovered in the State Paper Office. Why should he *then* have concealed the fact that he *now* vouchsafes to tell us? Nay, more than this, Mr. Halliwell, in giving a printed fac-simile of the document in question, announced to the public that it was *discovered by* Mr. Collier; a statement which Mr. Collier has never contradicted until the moment when public attention is critically drawn to the subject.

---

* "The Minute in the Registers of the Privy Council (pointed out to us by Mr. Lemon) is this," &c. Again, "This new and valuable piece of information was pointed out to us by Mr. Lemon."

There is another point, too, in Mr. Lemon's Letter that calls for notice, as tending somewhat to impugn the accuracy of his memory in reference to these transactions. He is only "pretty confident," he says, that his father first brought this document under the notice of Mr. Collier; but he speaks positively, or at all events seems to do so, as to the fact that this document "was well known to his father and himself *before* Mr. Collier began his researches in the office." Now it seems no more than reasonable to suppose that if he is only "pretty confident" in the one case, he can hardly be *more* than "pretty confident" in the other, which is more distant in point of time, and dating from a period prior to the alleged commencement of Mr. Collier's researches at the State Paper Office in 1829; a period at which, if we are not much mistaken, Mr. Lemon had nothing whatever to do with the State Paper Office in an official capacity, he having resigned his situation there in 1825, at the direction of the Under Secretary of State, "in order that he might devote his time exclusively to the Commission for printing and publishing State Papers," to which he had been appointed Assistant Secretary. This office he held until 1835, in which year he was appointed Second Clerk in the State Paper Office.

Under these circumstances, without meaning the slightest offence to Mr. Lemon, we cannot but be of opinion that he has spoken somewhat too hastily upon subjects which could hardly have come within his knowledge; viz., the existence of one document in particular, out of very many thousands, at a certain period of time, upwards of thirty years ago, the period of Mr. Collier's first admission into the State Paper Office; if indeed his letter can be construed to speak positively as to the latter point, which, after all, seems somewhat uncertain. Mr. Lemon, doubtless, is speaking the truth to the best of his belief; but not one iota beyond this can we admit.

To revert once more to the *Edinburgh* Reviewer, and *his* opinions on the "Players' Petition." Somewhat to our surprise, he boldly asserts (p. 484) that "the authenticity of the paper (the Players' Petition) is still maintained by the best authorities in the State Paper Office to be equal to that of any other document in the collection; and this opinion is curiously confirmed by the fact, that there are spots of corrosion by rust in the paper, which have eaten away not only the paper, *but the ink*, showing that the *writing*, as well as the paper, *is old.* The handwriting is not only not the handwriting of the Corrector, but it is of an essentially different character and period."

In the space of ninety words it is hardly possible to string together so many inaccuracies. In the first place, there is abundant reason for denying that " the authenticity of the paper is still maintained by the best authorities in the State Paper Office." Of the three Assistant Keepers of Public Records at the State Paper Branch Office, Mr. Lechmere, the chief, has hitherto declined to offer any opinion at all upon the subject; Mr. Lemon himself can at most be said to have expressed only by *implication* his belief in its genuineness; while the remaining Assistant Keeper, Mr. Hans Claude Hamilton, has stated his conviction that the so-called "Players' Petition" is an indubitable forgery.

Again, it is not the fact that " there are spots of corrosion by rust in the paper, which have eaten away not only the paper but the ink"; though, if there were such, it would point to an exactly opposite conclusion, as we could convince the Reviewer in two minutes, by affording him ocular demonstration. Further than this, our belief is, that the liquid with which the document was written was not what is commonly called 'ink,' or, at all events, the ink in use at that period. We admit that the paper is old, a century, perhaps, older than the writing; and as to the writing, if it is not that of the " Old Corrector," it is a very happy imitation of it, and bears a strong resemblance to that of some of the papers at Bridgewater House.

In the last place, the Reviewer commits an egregious error in reference to this subject (one that he might have avoided if he had only consulted so common a book as the " Royal Calendar " for 1859), in alleging, when making mention of the State Paper Office at Westminster, and the Record Office at the Rolls House, that, although under one head, " each department has its own staff of superior and subordinate officers, and its own distinct class of archives." This is not the fact; they are not distinct. The State Paper Office is only a branch of the Public Record Office, and the Deputy Keeper of the Public Records is the chief officer of the State Paper Branch, the whole being under his direction and management. He is, in fact, the responsible *Custos* of all the documents in the State Paper Branch, as well as in the Public Record Office itself. The Assistant Keepers located at the Public Record Office, are equally Assistant Keepers of the Branch at the State Paper Office, and *vice versâ*. Even more than this, the two offices have not their distinct archives. Both contain State Papers; though the Public Record Office contains, probably, the larger number of the two.

It is therefore a fallacy for the Reviewer to assert as he does that the officers of the State Paper Office were excluded from the official inquiry as to the Players' Petition; in addition to which, as already stated, Mr. Lechmere has, from the very first, declined to give an opinion as to the genuineness of this document. Mr. Lemon, too, had the opportunity, when he wrote his letter to the *Athenæum*, of distinctly stating his opinion as to the genuineness of the paper, but he forbore to do so.

As Mr. Collier and his supporters, however (notwithstanding the contradiction previously noticed), seem to hesitate at maintaining that the Players' Petition is genuine, it would be little better than a work of supererogation to prove that it is spurious. We therefore content ourselves with asserting that, be it original or copy, it was not written in the reign of Elizabeth or of James the First,—reigns which, of course, we particularly mention, because the handwriting is ostensibly an imitation of the handwriting of that period, and the context is intended to bear reference to the first of them. The orthography of the petition, the ink or pigment in which it is written, are not of those reigns, and the writing itself is tainted with clerical anachronisms ; while the paper is, to all appearance, the fly-leaf cut out of a book, and certainly would never have been used either for an original Petition to the Council, or for an official copy of one. These assertions the officers of the State Paper Office, it is believed, will not be disposed to contradict. As yet they have shown no inclination to do so— (for even supposing Mr. Lemon's memory to be accurate in every respect, his evidence goes no way whatever towards establishing the genuineness* of the document),—though, on the other hand, the reserve shown by them on this point (with the exception of Mr. H. C. Hamilton), is not unlikely to be misconstrued as seeming to give countenance to the statements circulated in reference to the great literary value of this spurious production. That they entertain such an opinion in reference to it, it would really be an ill compliment to suppose; but if so, why did they not, immediately upon reading the certificate impugning the genuineness of the document, send to the Master of the Rolls a counter-certificate, declaring their own belief in its genuineness, and protesting against such a certificate being appended until further consideration had been given to the subject? Why, in such case, have they allowed Mr. Collier's assertions to be called in question, and himself defrauded of that testimony, whatever its value, to which he has a right at their hands, if they believe in its genuineness? This, if ever there was one, is a matter in which the semblance even of a mistake should not be allowed to exist.

This subject leads us incidentally to the consideration of another matter that has grown out of the question of the genuineness of this document; the graceless and improper insinuations that have been recently put forth by one or two Reviewers, to the effect that the Master of the Rolls has made himself a party, in appearance or by implication, in a personal attack upon a private individual.

What are the simple facts of the case? A complaint was made to the Master of the Rolls that one of the Public Records in his charge was of a suspicious character. He directed an inquiry to be made into the matter. He did no more than this; and he certainly could do no less; indeed the country had a right to demand that, in virtue of his office, he should institute such an inquiry. Had he acted otherwise than he did, we do not hesitate to say that he would singularly have failed in the performance of his duty as Keeper of the Public Records.

---

* The *Edinburgh Review* (p. 455) thinks proper to say of this document, in reference, we presume, to Mr. Lemon's Letter, " Its *authenticity* has since been confirmed by evidence which appears to us to be irresistible." Either the Reviewer must be a man very easily satisfied in point of evidence, or he must be totally ignorant what the word "*authenticity*" means.

Of course, it did not lie within his own province to act as judge in a matter of this description. He therefore appointed a committee for the purpose, consisting of gentlemen whose daily study, for more than half their lives, has been the handwriting of the last six or eight centuries. These gentlemen came to the conclusion that the document was spurious, and gave their certificate accordingly; this the Master of the Rolls directed to be appended thereto, in order that the present inquiry might not be lost to memory, should the same question ever arise in future. This certificate did not charge, nor was it intended that it should charge, Mr. Collier, or any other person, either with fabricating the document or with inserting it among the Public Records. It merely stated that, in the opinion of the persons there named, the writing was spurious,—a dictum that neither Mr. Collier nor Mr. Lemon has since attempted to repudiate.

On this point, however, it is quite unnecessary to enlarge; and we should be loth to bear the semblance even of obtruding ourselves upon the reader as defending one whose high and unassailable character needs no defence. Even the little that has been said is based solely upon a determination that the truth shall be spoken, and that the public shall not be hoodwinked by insinuation or misled by a distortion of facts.

There yet remains to be noticed another fact connected with the Players' Petition,—we mean the loss of the Memorial which, Mr. Collier states, was appended to it when he last saw it. We do not require Mr. Collier to explain this loss; but we certainly do think that the officers of the State Paper Branch Office should do so. Mr. Collier says that the authenticity of this Memorial has never been questioned; perhaps not; but until it is produced and subjected to examination, it will be as well perhaps to withhold implicit confidence in its genuineness.

While on the subject of documents belonging to, or said to belong, to the State Paper Office, we would direct public attention to the disappearance of two other documents to which Mr. Collier has referred.—(1.) The Petition to the Privy Council from James Burbage and others in 1576, printed by Mr. Collier in his *" Annals of the Stage,"*

i. 227. (2.) Lord Pembroke's Letter, dated 27th August 1624. In reference to this last document, we have a Calendar made by Mr. Kempe, some twenty years since, of the papers of that period then in the State Paper Office. This Calendar has been lately printed by Mrs. Everett Green, and it makes no mention of this document; so that the paper must have been lost or removed more than twenty years ago, and apparently we have no memorial of its existence since it was used by Mr. Collier.

So much, then, for four documents made use of by Mr. Collier which he asserts were in the State Paper Office when he published his volume. One is positively declared, on no slight authority, to be spurious, and three others are now not forthcoming,—a curious coincidence, to say the least of it, and one that demands inquiry.

We now proceed to some examination of the papers alleged to have been discovered by Mr. Collier among the MSS. of the Earl of Ellesmere, in the Library at Bridgewater-house. They consist of the seven following documents, bearing reference to the life and times of Shakespeare :—

1. A paper " For the avoiding of the Play-house in the Blacke Friers."
2. A Letter of the poet Daniell.
3. A Certificate of the Players of the Blackfriars Theatre in reply to certain complaints.
4. The opinions of the two Chief Justices of either Bench concerning the jurisdiccõn, authoritie, and liberties claymed by the cittizens of London, within the precincte of the late dissolved howses of the White and Black Fryers of London, delivered the xxviith of Januarie 1579.
5. An Order to Robert Daborne and others to provide children for Her Majesty's Revels (dated 4th January 1609).
6. A copy of a letter from H. S. in favour " of the poore Players of the Black fryers."
7. Mainwaring's Account.

" The moment I discovered them," says Mr. Collier, speaking of these papers, " I carried them to the Earl of Ellesmere (then Lord Francis Leveson Gower), and read them to him.

At his lordship's instance I copied them, and left both originals and copies with his lordship."

The particulars of his discovery Mr. Collier afterwards communicated to his friend, Mr. Thomas Amyot, in the following words:—" When first I obtained permission to look through the Bridgewater MSS. in detail, I conjectured that it would be nearly impossible to turn over so many State Papers and such a bulk of correspondence, private and official, without meeting with something illustrative of the subject to which I have devoted so many years; but I certainly never anticipated being so fortunate as to obtain particulars so new, curious, and important, regarding a poet who, above all others, ancient or modern, native or foreign, has been the object of admiration. When I took up the copy of Lord Southampton's Letter, and glanced over it hastily, I could scarcely believe my eyes to see such names as Shakespeare and Burbage in connection in a manuscript of the time. There was a remarkable coincidence also in the discovery, for it happened on the anniversary of Shakespeare's birth and death. I will not attempt to describe my joy and surprise; and I can only liken it to the unexpected gratification I experienced two or three years ago, when I turned out, from some ancient depositories of the Duke of Devonshire, the original designs of Inigo Jones, not only for the scenery, but for the dresses and characters of the different masques by Ben Jonson, Campion, Townsend, &c. presented at court in the reigns of our First James and Charles. The sketches were sometimes accompanied by explanations in the handwriting of the great artist, a few of which incidentally illustrate Shakespeare, who, however, was never employed for any of these royal entertainments. Annexed to one of the drawings was the following written description, from whence we learn how the actor of the part of Falstaff was usually habited in the time of Shakespeare:— ' Like a Sir Jon Falstaff: in a roabe of russet, quite low, with a great belley, like a swolen man, long moustacheos, the sheows [shoes] shorte, and out of them great toes like naked feete: buskins to sheaw a great swolen leg. A cupp coming fourth like a beake—a great head and balde, and a little cap alla Venetiane greasy—a rodd and a scroule of parchment.* ' "

* " New Facts regarding the Life of Shakspeare," in a Letter to Thomas Amyot, from J. Payne Collier, 1835.

" It is somewhat remarkable," says Mr. Hamilton, " that neither this drawing, nor the description of Falstaff, is to be found in the Shakespeare Society's volume, edited by J. R. Planché, Esq., from the Duke of Devonshire's Library.* The language of this ' description ' is, to say the least, suspicious." The orthography, Mr. Hamilton might have added, is conclusive against its authenticity.

Mr. Collier in this letter, it will be observed, dwells emphatically on the value of these documents ; but makes no observation on the handwriting that could raise a suspicion as to their genuineness, while he enters into all the particulars of their being found in bundles of MSS. which had probably never been examined since the days of Chancellor Ellesmere ; —a circumstance, he considers, which tells strongly in their favour.

To proceed, however, to an examination of the above-mentioned documents individually.

1. "For the avoiding of the Play-house in the Blacke Friers."†

---

* Mr. Hamilton, in his "*Inquiry*," p. 103, has called marked attention to the spurious character of a MS. volume of Ballads stated by Mr. Collier to be in his possession, and in a handwriting of the time of the Commonwealth, but which, from the internal evidence of the ballads published, as well as from a fac-simile of the handwriting of a portion of one of them, he pronounces to be unmistakeable modern forgeries. Mr. Collier has silently passed over Mr. Hamilton's challenge to him to produce the book, even though his supporter, the *Edinburgh* Reviewer, declares that in this particular instance Mr. Collier must be either deceiver or deceived.

" Mr. Collier," says the Reviewer, " published in 1839, as an extract from an alleged manuscript volume in his possession, a trashy ballad called *The Inchanted Island*, the plot of which is similar to that of *The Tempest*. Mr. Douce, he says, shook his venerable head, and called it one of the most beautiful ballads he had ever read ; which must have been in some strange fit of after-dinner enthusiasm. Mr. Collier conjectures that it was written between 1642 and 1660. It has been fac-similed for Mr. Halliwell. Mr. Hamilton says that the writing is suspicious ; of which we say nothing. But we fully agree with him that the intrinsic character of the verses themselves by no means serves to allay these suspicions. It would take a good deal to persuade us that lines in which it is said of a magician that—

' Snooth to say, in dangerous hour
He had some more than human power ;'

in which a lady's hair is described as ' like to sunlit gold;' and in which it is said of a father that 'his little Ida's morning smile made him forget his woe'—were by any very ancient ballad-monger. But we know not whether Mr. Collier in this particular instance is either deceived or deceiver." (*Edinb. Review*, No. 226, p. 483.)

† Printed in Mr. Hamilton's "*Inquiry*," p. 110.

This paper is cleverly executed, and might at first sight pass for a copy of a genuine document; but certainly neither for an original nor for a contemporaneous copy. The more, however, it is examined, the more suspicious it appears. The ink is not what the ink of that period was, and the paper has been evidently the fly-leaf of a book.

No one, probably, will contend that this piece is the original; and if it is not the original, it becomes of interest to know where the original is, and how a copy of this document should have been found among papers having no connexion whatever with those belonging to the Egerton family.

This circumstance not improbably influenced the late Lord Ellesmere, when he insisted on Mr. Collier keeping the document he had found, as it was no necessary part of the Egerton family documents.

2. A Letter * " To the Right Honorable Sir Thomas Egerton, Knight, Lord Keeper of the Great Seale of England, from S. Daniell."

The statement that this is an original letter sent by Daniell to Sir Thomas Egerton is preposterous, and, to say the least, must have been made in utter ignorance; for neither in the handwriting, the ink, nor in any other particular does it bear any characteristic of the reign of Elizabeth.

If, on the other hand, it is asserted that it is a copy, how comes it that the copy of a letter addressed to the founder of this noble house should have been preserved, and neither the original preserved nor the fact of its having existed in any way recorded?

3. A Certificate † of the Poore Playeres, being sharers in the Blacke Fryers Playhouse in November 1589.

This is written on a slip of paper, evidently taken from a book. Mr. Collier suggests that it passed into the hands

---

* Printed in Mr. Hamilton's " *Inquiry,*" p. 111.
† Printed in Mr. Hamilton's "*Inquiry*," p. 113.

of Lord Ellesmere, then Attorney General, and that it has been preserved among his papers ever since. This, however, must be an error, for Popham was Attorney General at that time, and not Sir Thomas Egerton.

The document itself is of a most suspicious character; and it is impossible not to agree with Mr. Collier that "it seems strange that this testimonial should have come from the players themselves. We should rather have expected that they would have procured a certificate from some disinterested parties."

The fabricator of the document, however, must have had some reason of his own for making it in this form, which, of course, it is not for others to pretend to divine. Be this, however, as it may, no one who has the slightest pretensions to a knowledge of the handwriting of the reign of Elizabeth, would hesitate for an instant in condemning the paper from the writing alone; and we canot forbear expressing our surprise that any person should venture to call this document an original of the 16th century.

5. The opinions of the two Chief Justices of either Bench concerning the jurisdiccōn, authoritie, and liberties claymed by the cittizens of London, within the precincte of the late dissolved howses of the White and Black Fryers of London, delivered the xxvii[th] of Januarie 1579.

This piece is written in the Gothic hand of the 16th century, and is supposed by gentlemen of acknowledged skill in such matters to be a genuine document. Still, after a close examination, to us its genuineness seems questionable at least. Be this the case or not, it certainly is not an original, but only a copy.

5. An Order * to Robert Daborne and others, to provide children for Her Majesty's Revels (dated 4th January 1609).

This document is perhaps the most transparent fabrication of any that has been put forth as an original. As a fac-simile

---

* Printed in Hamilton's "*Inquiry*," p. 114.

of it has been published in Mr. Hamilton's *"Inquiry,"* the reader has the opportunity of forming his own opinion ; and, if he has any knowledge of the handwriting of the reign of James I. he cannot fail to condemn it at once.

6. *Copia vera* of a Letter* from H. S. in favour of the poore Players of the Black fryers.

This piece professes to be only a true copy (*copia vera*), and has excited considerable attention.   It has no date, and is not addressed to any one,— a somewhat extraordinary circumstance, seeing that it is attested as *copia vera*.   For how can it be *"copia vera"* unless the name of the person addressed is also given?   The fabricator of the paper must have felt this difficulty, but was at a loss how to remedy it.   He needed some such document probably to supply a link in a certain chain that he was weaving, and he knew that the less definite the document should be, the smaller the chance of detection.   He knew, in fact, that there would have been considerable risk in affixing either the date, the name of the writer, or the name of the person addressed.   Mr. Collier, however, when publishing the document, thus gets over the difficulty : " We may conclude," he says, " that the original was not addressed to Lord Ellesmere, or it would have been found in the depository of his papers, and not merely a transcript of it."   This argument, however, would seem hardly tenable, for how is it that the Lord Keeper did not preserve the original of the letter from the poet Daniell, which was addressed to him ?   Why should he have preserved the copy among his family papers, and not the original ?

" But," continues Mr. Collier, " a copy of it may have been furnished to the Lord Chancellor, in order to give him some information respecting the characters of the parties upon whose cause he was called upon to adjudicate." What cause ?—certainly none in the Chancery ; of that we have very good evidence.   But why should a letter addressed to some nameless person by an anonymous writer, signing himself H. S., be sent to the Lord Keeper ?   Mr. Collier supposes, though without a shadow of support, that the letter was written by the Earl of Southampton, and was sent by

---

the nameless person to the Lord Keeper merely to enlighten him as to the deserts of Shakespeare and Burbage! The idea cannot be entertained, for a moment even.

7. Rewardes to the vaulters, players, and dauncers. Of this x^{li} to Burbadge's players: for Othello, lxiii^{li}, xviii^s, x^d. Rewarde to Mr. Lillye's man, which brought the lotterye box to Harefield, x^{li}.

This document professes to be an account of the expenditure of the Lord Keeper of the Great Seal (signed by Arthur Mainwaring, who appears to have been his auditor) for the reception of Queen Elizabeth, on her visit to him at Harefield, in the beginning of August 1602. It furnishes a fact which, if it could be relied upon, would to a certain extent settle the question as to the date of the first appearance of the Tragedy of " Othello,"—a disputed point; some critics assigning it to 1604, others to 1611.

Mr. Collier produces this Account to prove that Burbadge's Players received from the Lord Keeper 63l. 18s. 10d. for playing Othello before the Queen, on Her Majesty's visit to Harefield, in August 1602; consequently, that the play must have been written and performed in London before that date.* Unfortunately, however, the paper upon which Mr. Collier rests his proof must be condemned as spurious. The difference between it and the others in the same volume of manuscripts, signed by Arthur Mainwaring, which are unquestionably genuine, is striking; and, although it is written on paper similar to the others, the writing, the ink, and the signature equally condemn it at once.

Speaking of these documents, Mr. Collier says,† " I admit, without reserve, that the weakest part of my case relates to the finding of Shakespeare documents among the late Earl of Ellesmere's MSS., at Bridgewater-house ; and why is it the weakest part of my case? For this sole reason, that I never could have had any direct corroboration of my own testimony as to the discovery of them. Nobody was with

* See Mr. Collier's " Introduction to Othello," vii. 493.
† " Reply to Mr. Hamilton's ' Inquiry,' " p. 34.

me at the precise moment, although the noble owner of the papers had been in the room only a few minutes before."

We agree with Mr. Collier, that it is unfortunate that no other person was present when he found these papers; and even more unfortunate is it that he never is able to cite the testimony of any living person as being present at the moment of any one of his discoveries.

But to follow Mr. Collier a step further.—"Mr. Hamilton," he says, "boldly begging the whole question, styles them ' the Bridgewater Shakespeare forgeries.' They may be ' forgeries,' but at that time it never entered my head that they could be so; and at that time I had never heard the fact, since mentioned, that Stevens had formerly been admitted into the rooms which held both the books and the manuscripts. I do not believe that he had any more hand in the forgeries than the Rev. H. J. Todd, with whom I once conversed about the papers, and who had, as I understood, for some years filled the office of librarian."

To say the least of it, this is a most unworthy insinuation. To remove suspicion from himself, Mr. Collier, by a sort of negative pregnant, would impugn the honour of two gentlemen long since deceased, and unable therefore to speak for themselves.

Every one who knows anything of the world, knows full well that the man who forges a document produces and makes it public in order that he himself may reap the benefit of his forgery; that it is "*sic vos non vobis*" least of all with a person of such crooked tendencies as these. Had either Stevens or Todd forged them, he would most assuredly have drawn the attention of the public to them, and would not have allowed another person to reap the benefit of his labours. Mr. Collier was both the discoverer of these documents and the editor of them as genuine; while, from his own admission, it would seem that he would not be very reluctant now to admit them to be forgeries.

But why is Mr. Collier indignant with Mr. Hamilton for calling these documents forgeries? He exhibited no such indignation in 1853 against Mr. Halliwell, who not only denounced them as such, but gave a fac-simile of one of the documents in question, with the view of substantiating his position.

"Fortunately for the interests of truth," says Mr. Halliwell, "indications of forgery are detected in trifling circumstances, that are almost invariably neglected by the inventor, however ingeniously the deception be contrived. Were it not for this, the search for historical truth would yield results sufficiently uncertain to deter the most enthusiastic inquirer from pursuing the investigation." To which he adds: "It is clearly Mr. Collier's duty, as a lover of truth, to have the originals carefully scrutinized by the best judges of the day."

An ordinarily sensitive man would surely, upon a challenge like this, have adopted such a course, rather than that a shadow of suspicion should rest upon his name. Mr. Collier forbore to do so; on the contrary, he has remained silent and inactive until now, when he assumes an air of indignation, and rises, armed at all points with insinuations, sneers, and insults, directed against every person who ventures to come forward to investigate, in the name of truth and learning, a great literary question. Mr. Collier, if conscious of being above all blame, ought to have been thankful to Mr. Hamilton for affording him, in whatever spirit, the opportunity of dispelling any suspicion that might lurk in the minds of Shakespearian scholars that he had brought before the literary world numberless supposititious emendations of the text of Shakespeare, and some equally supposititious facts connected with his life.

Having thus cursorily noticed the spurious Shakespearian papers in the Ellesmere Collection, we now come to the Dulwich documents of a like character, to which Mr. Collier has called the attention of the literary world. They consist of four papers, three of which are undoubtedly anything but genuine; and the fourth, known as "Mrs. Alleyn's Letter" to her husband, has been treated by Mr. Collier in a most extraordinary manner in the use which he has made of it. We take Mrs. Alleyn's Letter first.

Mr. Collier professes* to give the world a correct copy of this letter; but, on examination, his copy has been found

---

* *Memoirs of Alleyn*, p. 62.

to differ, in by far its most material points, from the original. In his version not only have words been left out and others inserted (we do not here allude to several inaccuracies of minor importance), but one entire passage—a most important one, containing a mention of William Shakespeare—has been introduced!

Subjoined is a correct copy of that portion of the letter to which we allude, accompanied by Mr. Collier's version of it. In italics are given the words, and fragments of words, which Mr. Collier has omitted, and in small capitals those which appear in their place. It will thus be seen at a glance, that there can be no mistake about the matter, but that in reality the passage in question does not exist, and never could have existed.

> "Aboute a weeke agoe there [cam]e a youthe who said he was
> Mr. Frauncis Chalo[ner]s man . . . . ld have borrow[e]d x⁵ to
> bought have ˏthings for [h]is *Mr.* . . . . *t hym*
> *Cominge without* . . . *token* . . . . *d*
> *I would have* . . . .
> *& I bene su* . . . .
> and inquire after the fellow and said he had lent hym a horse. I
> us feare me he gulled hym, thoughe he gulled not ˏ. The youthe
> what was a prety youthe and handsom in appayrell, we know not ˏbecame
> of him Mr. Bromffeild commends hym : he was heare yesterdaye. Nicke
> and Jeames be well, and commend them, so dothe Mr. Cooke and his woife
> in the kyndest sorte, and so once more in the hartiest manner
> farwelle
>
> "Your faithfull and lovinge weife
> "JOANE ALLEYNE."

> "Aboute a weeke a goe there came a youthe who said he was
> Mr. Frauncis Chaloner who would have borrowed xˡⁱ to
> have bought things for * * * AND SAID HE WAS KNOWN
> UNTO YOU, AND MR. SHAKESPEARE OF THE GLOBE, WHO CAME
> * * * SAID HE KNEWE HYM NOT, ONLY HE HEARDE OF HYM THAT HE WAS
> A ROGE * * * SO HE WAS GLADE WE DID NOT LEND HIM
> THE MONNEY * * * RICHARD JOHNES [WENT] TO SEEKE
> and inquire after the fellow, and said he had lent hym a horse. I
> feare me he gulled hym, thoughe he gulled not us. The youthe
> was a prety youthe, and hansom in appayrell : we knowe not what became
> of hym. Mr. Benfield commendes hym; he was heare yesterdaye. Nicke
> and Jeames be well, and comend them : so doth Mr. Cooke and his wiefe
> in the kyndest sorte, and so once more in the hartiest manner
> farwell.
>
> "Your faithfull and lovinge *wiefe.*
> "JOANE ALLEYNE."

It is not our intention to notice all the inaccuracies of Mr. Collier's version, but a few only of the most striking. The reader who is desirous of seeing them in their totality may consult Mr. Hamilton's "*Inquiry*," pp. 91–93, where all the variations between Mr. Collier's text and the original letter at Dulwich College are printed in italics.

In the second line, 10*s.* has been misread as 10*l.*, a thing that certainly betrays no little ignorance, as 10*l.* in those days would have equalled about 60*l.* of our present money

A strange youth calls on Mrs. Alleyn, and asks the loan of 10*l.* as coolly as he would have asked for as many pence!

But the really unpardonable discrepancy in this case is the introduction of the following words,—words which are not, and never by any possibility could have been, in the original:—" *and said he was known unto you, and Mr. Shakespeare of the Globe, who came . . . said he knewe hym not, only he hearde of hym that he was a roge . . . . so he was glade we did not lend him the monney . . . . Richard Johnes [went] to seeke ;*" while not one of the ten words in this place, which really do exist and are plainly visible in the original document, is to be found in Mr. Collier's version.

The fact is indisputable that he has put fourteen lines in the space that in reality is occupied by thirteen only in the original; while the terminations of the third and fourth lines in the above extract are wholly changed, and nine words, which are distinctly legible at the beginning of the fourth, fifth, and sixth lines, are suppressed.

In defending himself against the charges brought against him in reference to this letter, Mr. Collier, it seems hardly too much to say, is at once evasive and illogical. He says:* " Now the question is, and the only question of the slightest importance (though that is in truth of little moment), whether the name of ' Mr. Shakespeare, of the Globe,' occurred in the most rotten and fragmentary part of the letter at the time when I copied it. Whether it did or did not, is not of the smallest interest as regards the biography of our poet."

Mr. Collier is correct, no doubt, in saying that the question is not of the smallest interest as regards the biography of our poet; but, in reference to the trustworthiness and accuracy of Mr. Collier, it cannot but be of the greatest importance that the words should be where he has alleged that he had seen them to be.

He further states :—" I do not deny that it is possible I misread some utterly unimportant letters and words."

---

* " *Reply,*" p. 48.

Unfortunately, however, not only has Mr. Collier misread what he thinks proper to call "unimportant" words, but he has omitted several which are evident to even an unskilled eye, and has inserted words, indeed whole sentences, where they never could have occurred. But to proceed with his statement. He says: "I am absolutely certain that 'Mr. Shakespeare, of the Globe,' was spoken of in it in the way I stated. Mr. Hamilton asserts that 'there is not the smallest trace of authority for any allusion to Shakespeare.' This may be very true; he is speaking of Mrs. Alleyn's letter in its present condition, but that is not the question. The question is, whether, when I saw the letter, some thirty or even more years ago, the name of 'Mr. Shakespeare, of the Globe,' was not to be traced."

Now, in answer to this, we maintain with Mr. Hamilton, and so must every other person who is possessed of eye-sight and common understanding, that not only is it not there now, but that it never could by any possibility have been in the place where Mr. Collier asserts it was; any more than that those words could have been added to the document since Mr. Collier saw it which have been omitted by him. Under these circumstances, if Mr. Collier could call twenty dead friends, in addition to the one he invokes,* it would make no difference in his favour; facts speak for themselves, and neither dead nor living can gainsay them.

Another link—one of circumstantial evidence—may be added to the argument already adduced. Malone, that careful Shakespearian critic and indefatigable inquirer, had the box of papers which contained this letter to look over and examine at his leisure. Surely, if he had discovered any allusion to William Shakespeare, whose very name would in his estimation have hallowed the paper whereon it was written, he would have made some note or mention of it; but we turn to him in vain for corroborative evidence of Mr. Collier's assertion.

A few more words in reference to Mrs. Alleyn's letter. Mr. Collier states† that he carefully enclosed the letter in paper after he had copied it, and that either he or his now deceased friend wrote on the outside of the paper, that within was a document of value, which should not be roughly handled; and he asks whether it is likely he would have done so had he purposely misstated the import and contents of a letter that was in a state of ruinous decay? Would not the natural course for him to pursue have been to have left the letter as it was, in the hope that when it was next seen and consulted, as much of it might have disappeared as possible? He further asks,—If he had misrepresented the contents of the crumbling relic, what was to prevent his rubbing away a little more of the old paper, and who then would have been able to detect the trick he had played? * Now, the only answer to this is, that true it is, there is in the tin box at Dulwich College a sheet of paper enclosing this identical document, with a memorandum written in pencil to the above effect; but, singular to relate, this memorandum is not in the handwriting of Mr. Collier, nor yet of his friend Mr. Amyot, as the writer of the article in *Notes and Queries* has inconsiderately asserted.

A fac-simile of that portion of the letter which is the subject of the present discussion was made by that careful and expert artist, Mr. Fairholt; and which agrees *verbatim et literatim* with the fac-simile made by Mr. Nethercliffe, Junior, as given in Mr. Hamilton's " Inquiry."

Too much, it may possibly be thought, has been said upon this branch of our subject; but it is one of so much importance in the enquiry, that it could hardly have been dismissed in fewer words.

To proceed, however, with the other documents at Dulwich College.

The next document that calls for notice is a paper in verse, consisting of seventeen lines, called by Mr. Collier

---

* It is somewhat strange that, in his earlier answer to Mr. Hamilton, which appeared in the *Athenæum*, Mr. Collier makes no allusion to the circumstances of his having placed the " crumbling relic " in a sheet of paper and indorsed it with the caution we have here mentioned. The Editor of the *Athenæum* was the first to assert in print that the indorsement is in Mr. Collier's handwriting.

" The Players' Challenge," and commencing "Sweet Nedde, now wynne an other wager." It was printed by him in 1841, in his " *Memoirs of Alleyn,*" p. 18.

A cursory examination of this paper must convince most persons at all acquainted with handwriting of the sixteenth and seventeenth centuries that it is spurious. It is, however, neatly written, and would not improbably deceive a person inexperienced in palæography. Mr. Collier says :*
" I have no particular recollection of the manner in which it is written ; but, contrary to what Mr. Hamilton says, that it is ' executed with singular dexterity,' it now seems to me that the re-duplication of consonants, and other points of orthography in it, might possibly - raise suspicion." Mr. Collier is right. The facts that he mentions do raise suspicion,—a suspicion which we are surprised did not cross his mind when he published the document, and which is not confined to the orthography alone.

The Letter from Marston, the dramatist, to Hensloe, also printed by Mr. Collier in his " *Memoirs of Alleyn,*" p. 154, is another of these Dulwich documents. " It refers," says Mr. Collier, " to a play by Marston, on the subject of Columbus, of which we have no other authority." In this letter, pencil-marks are visible, faintly indeed, for the most part, though in one or two instances they are pretty distinct ; and not so very faint are they but that in them nearly every word of the letter can be distinctly traced. As to the letter itself, written in ink, it is evidently penned in imitation of Marston's hand. To a practised eye, however, the difference between the genuine handwriting of Marston and this imitation is quite perceptible ; and there cannot be the slightest doubt that the document is a fabrication.

The next paper at Dulwich which calls for notice, is a " List of Players," in which Shakespeare's name occurs. It is printed in the " *Memoirs of Alleyn,*" p. 68, and Mr. Collier himself admits that it is in a different ink from that used in the document to which it is appended. The document to which the List of Players is attached is genuine, no doubt, and is noticed by Malone in his " *Inquiry*" (1796); but he

---

* " *Reply,*" p. 54.

makes no allusion whatever to any List of Players being thereto annexed. However, Mr. Collier, when in 1841 he published the List in question, suggested that Malone's reason for passing it over was, that he intended to use the information contained in it in his Life of Shakespeare which he did not live to publish.

Mr. Collier's suggestion is by no means satisfactory. It seems little short of incredible that Malone should have passed over such a remarkable paper without some notice of it, if he really had seen it. His was no hurried inspection of the Dulwich papers, for they remained in his hands for several years. It is more than probable, then, that he saw this document many a time, and if so, he could not have overlooked the List of Players attached to it. Be this, however, as it may, the handwriting proclaims the " List of Players " to be spurious.

We cannot dismiss the name of Malone without calling attention to another subject ; one that certainly seems to demand some explanation at Mr. Collier's hands, if he would prevent the literary world from judging him by his own apparent estimate of honour and morality. In pp. 46, 47, of his " *Reply* " to Mr. Hamilton, we find the following passage— (the italics are our own) :—

" Let it be borne in mind that the documents which Malone here and elsewhere refers to were, in fact, the property of the Master, Warden, and Fellows of Dulwich College ; that Malone had *quietly* taken possession of them ; that they remained in his hands for several years ; that *he did exactly what he liked with them ;* that he *cut off signatures* of old dramatists and players, to place them on the title-pages of his own books ; and that *he or others mutilated* ' *Henslowe's Diary*,' in such a way that some of the most valuable portions are entirely lost. Even the books the title-pages of which he decorated with the old autographs, had belonged to Dulwich College ; for *he contrived to persuade* the Master, Warden, and Fellowes of that day that old plays and old poetry did not half so well become their shelves as the musty divinity, dull chronicles, and other volumes of the same sort, which he substituted ; hence the bulk of his collection. And he must have *chuckled amazingly at his success in persuading unsuspecting people to make an exchange of works, which would sell for hundreds of pounds, for others not worth as many shillings.* So of the manuscripts ; they seem to have allowed Malone to carry away such as he pleased, to keep them as long as he pleased, *and to return such as he pleased, in the state which he pleased.* Some that *he did not return* found their way again to their old home, after his death ; and it is not very long since the College, most properly, bought back a bundle of papers that must have originally come out of its archives."

Now, if we know anything as to the force and meaning of the English language, this is a circumstantial description of the thoughts and actions of none other than a violator of the ordinary ties of honour, friendship, and integrity ; in other words, a swindler and a rogue. But be this as it may, it is Mr. Collier's deliberate description of the doings and dealings—so far as Dulwich College was concerned — of Edward Malone.

We next turn to page 53 of Mr. Collier's " *Reply*,"—the italics again our own.

" If any of the documents returned to Dulwich College after Malone's death appear to have been tampered with, I most distinctly acquit him of any such misconduct. Whatever I may be in the opinion of my adversaries, I feel sure that he was *a man of honour and principle.*"

How does Mr. Collier reconcile this passage with the distinct statements and the downright assertions as to Edward Malone made by him in the passages that have been previously quoted ? If the conduct there imputed to him is in any way reconcileable with Mr. Collier's code of " honour and principle," all that we have to add is, that we are far from surprised at the phase this most unhappy controversy has now assumed.

It is necessary, before concluding these remarks, to bestow some notice upon an argument, if, indeed, an argument it can properly be called, which is prominently put forward by Mr. Collier in his " *Reply*," and, indeed, repeated by him again and again.

This is the gist of his charge; that his opponents, and more particularly what he calls the MS. Department of the British Museum, of which he styles Mr. Hamilton " the mouthpiece," entertain certain feelings of personal enmity against himself. As to the motive for making this charge, it is obvious. All persons, particularly the English public, have an instinctive love of fair play ; and if it could be shown that a man, entertaining feelings of personal animosity against another, had taken advantage of a plausible opportunity for gratifying his malignity and resentment, the feelings of the community would assuredly be strongly enlisted in favour of the object of the attack. Still stronger would that feeling be, if the person attacked were an aged man of literary acquirements and unblemished reputation; and least of all would such a violation of propriety be tolerated, if committed by one literary man against another.

It is not too much to say that such assailants, and under such circumstances, would find disfavour from all ; their arguments would be unwillingly listened to, and their conclusions reluctantly admitted ; while any plausible answer in excuse would be eagerly accepted, nor would the public be very eager to inquire into the exact balance of merits in such a contest as this.

Still, however, in reference to such a case as the present, the public would, in equal justice, deem itself bound to distinguish between the hostility which is the result of the indignation natural to honourable men, who, after a fair and impartial investigation, have had the suspicion forced upon them that a series of literary deceptions had been committed, and *that* hostility, which, springing from a previously existing enmity, has seized a favourable occasion to inflict an injury upon a literary colleague.

In the former case a certain amount of hostility—not unmixed, perhaps, with different feelings—might be fairly supposed to be the natural and inevitable consequence of a suspicion, amounting to reasonable belief, that so grave an offence had been committed. For what graver offence could possibly be committed against the republic of letters than the forgery of documents and annotations connected with the name of a deceased writer, for every fact connected with whom the last century and a half have been athirst ?

proving a source of error and confusion to the literary world, and this, merely to gratify the fabricator's literary ambition, or to conduce to his profit.

An offence of this description unsettles literary questions, introduces distrust into the assertions of authors, compels the reader to test for himself the truth of everything he reads, and above all tends to lower the standard of English literary honesty in the eyes of the enlightened men of other nations. Well, then, might the literary men of England, and especially those connected with a department so peculiarly interested in such questions as is the MS. Department of the British Museum, feel indignant, if such a case, in their belief, were made out ; and as readily would the public excuse any one who had advocated the cause of what he sincerely believed to be the truth, with more than ordinary warmth.

Now, in reference to the language of his " *Reply*," Mr. Collier evidently had this distinction present to his mind; for he labours to persuade his readers, not so much that the articles recently written in reference to his Shakespearian discoveries contain marks of hostility, as that those articles are the result of a previously existing enmity. He feels that it is not sufficient for him to show that such a relation *now* exists between himself and those who impugn his statements, but that, in order to enlist the public in his favour, he must establish the fact that he is the object of a previously existing hostility, and that this is an occasion taken for its display.

And how does Mr. Collier prove this? Assuming its existence, and reasoning from it as from a fact that is undoubted and undeniable, he would evidently ascribe it to the literary reputation which he has acquired.

* In his " *Reply* "* to Mr. Hamilton, he says : " I have always striven to make myself as unobjectionable as I could, but even my small reputation, in an inferior department of letters, seems to excite envy ; and I foresaw, that when Lord Campbell, as a kind compliment to that reputation rather than to my merits, addressed to me his letter ' On the Legal Acquirements of Shakespeare,' it would materially tend to exasperate

---

* Page 6.

my enemies. It had not long been published before
Sir F. Madden, &c. wrote to the Duke of Devonshire, in
order to borrow the Perkins folio; and having procured it,
Mr. N. E. S. A. Hamilton 'seized the opportunity,' as he
himself expresses it, of subjecting it, with the aid of Sir
F. Madden and others, to the most rigorous examination."
He further ascribes the hostility of Sir F. Madden, as will be
seen, to other unintentional causes of offence,--supposed
neglect (pp. 11, 70), and services rendered on two occasions
(pp. 28, 29). Mr. Arnold also he assumes to be his personal enemy, and vaguely suggests that it is to something
that had passed between him and the father of that most
estimable and enlightened magistrate,* that he is indebted
for this enmity.

Occasionally, however, Mr. Collier seems to profess
himself at a loss to account for this unmerited hostility. At
one time he suggests that the cause of the enmity of the
Museum officials may have arisen from his not having
especially invited them to see the folio when he publicly
exhibited it; and then, in a similar spirit, he proceeds to say :
" I have been told, but I do not believe it, that Sir
F. Madden and his colleagues were irritated by this piece of
supposed neglect, and that they also took it ill that I presented the Perkins folio to the kindest, most condescending,
and most liberal of noblemen, instead of giving it to their
institution. When I placed it in the hands of the Duke of
Devonshire, I knew that for any literary purpose it would
be just as accessible,† and just as safe in his Grace's library
as in that of the British Museum." In another place‡ he
evidently seems inclined to ascribe their hostility to his
having been recommended to the Queen to fill the office of
Principal Librarian of the Museum. Again, he suggests that

---

* "If Mr. T. J. Arnold be the son of the late S. J. Arnold, the dramatist,
perhaps I can understand part of the cause of his undeserved animosity towards
me. It may be an entirely different, but not an indifferent person."—*Reply*,
page 7.

† This is a fallacy, seeing that as the Duke of Devonshire's Library was not
open to the public, while that of the British Museum was, the former could
not, for literary or any other purposes, be deemed as accessible as the latter.
Indeed, to place it in the Duke's Library was the very way to hide it from the
public view; for the Duke might with justice have refused the applications of
the literary public, a thing that neither Mr. Collier nor the Museum could
have done.

‡ "*Reply*," p. 30.

the officers of the Museum may possibly owe him * some ill-will for finding them work, in procuring three large cases of Bentinck MSS. from Germany; he thus having been " the innocent means of procuring for them occupation." In another place,† he says: "How and why the MS. authorities of the British Museum have been heated into such animosity towards me, I cannot pretend to explain. I was always on good terms with Sir F. Madden, whom I have known for more than a quarter of a century, and upon two occasions I was of service to him. Of one of them I can say no more; but of the other I may remark that it occurred within the last two or three years, and it was when he had involved himself in an awkward scrape, by purchasing MSS. which he ought to have known had been dishonestly come by. * * * *." " Some men can forget an injury, who never can forgive an obligation;" but still, he‡ " cannot for a moment suppose that Sir F. Madden and the younger officers of the Museum have taken any antipathy to him on that score."

The public, no doubt, will, equally with Mr. Collier, be unable from such causes as these to account for such hostility as he imputes to those gentlemen who have done no more than exert themselves to solve the question as to the genuineness of the annotations in the Devonshire folio,‖ and to prove the existence of certain forgeries in the shape of documents professing to contain the poet's name.

Should it be urged by Mr. Collier, in reference to these charges of preconceived hostility, that he requires nothing beyond what is contained in the publications against him to prove the truth of his assertion, this will not answer his purpose. It is a mere begging of the question, and in reality leaves the question wholly untouched. Is all this mere animosity? or is it the result of an enforced conviction that

---

* " *Reply*," p. 62.   † " *Reply*," p. 28.   ‡ " *Reply*," p. 30.
‖ So great an offence is this in Mr. Collier's eyes, that his insinuations as to unfair motives extend beyond the British shores. Speaking of the criticisms which appeared on the publication of " *Notes and Emendations*," he says :— " In Germany both it and I have been violently assailed by critics of every grade ; in some instances with a degree of personal rancour, for which I can only account on the supposition that I have unwarily, unwittingly, and sometimes unavoidably, neglected publications which have been sent to me as presents from their authors."

F

the writings and documents in question are forgeries? If the latter, which, for our own part, we are convinced really is the case, Mr. Collier's charges of hostility are a mere fallacy, and of course the question is left exactly where it was. That question is this: Does the evidence establish, first, that these documents are forged, these annotations modern? And, next: Is Mr. Collier, according to the existing evidence, so connected with them as to justify something more than mere doubt and hesitation on the part of careful and impartial investigators?

If we look abroad into the world, we shall find that the charge of hostility, derived in reality from the matter in question itself, but ascribed to preconceived enmity, is one of common occurrence. It is a matter of almost every-day experience for the losing party in a suit to say that some of the jurors were his enemies. The defendant in a Chancery suit is not uncommonly heard to express his surprise that the judge has shown such remarkable animosity towards him, and to profess himself at a loss to know what he could have possibly done to deserve or occasion it. A pertinent illustration of this will be familiar to the recollection of all who are well acquainted with the writings of the late Rev. Sydney Smith, who, having severely castigated certain of the States of the North American Union for the repudiation of their public debts,— their refusal, in fact, to pay either principal or interest of monies received by them, and of which the inhabitants of the State had received the advantage—was met by various answers; in most of which, however, was prominently put forward, by way of exordium, an expression of surprise as to what could be the cause or origin of all this hatred of our American brethren. Sydney Smith's reply is so very germane to a controversy of this description that we cannot but commend it to the notice of the reader.*

Possibly, however, too much may have been said on this point. Still, as Mr. Collier repeats it so often, and makes it so leading, indeed, so offensive a feature of his defence, a more elaborate notice of it may be justified than in reality would have been due to any real claims to notice that it possesses.

---

* *Miscellaneous Works of the Rev. Sydney Smith* (1859), vol. ii., p. 330.

For ourselves personally (and, indeed, for all those who have arrived at conclusions in this investigation similar to our own, so far as the opportunity has been afforded us of penetrating into their thoughts or motives,) we can honestly say that we disown any species of personal animosity against Mr. Collier.   Indeed, so far as we ourselves are concerned, we entertain more of another feeling than of the indignation which, as already observed, might naturally spring from a reasonable belief in the truthfulness of the charges made by Mr. Collier's opponents : but still, we feel ourselves bound to say that, convinced as we are that the documents in question are spurious, and the annotations in the folio of modern fabrication, and that Mr. Collier has by no means satisfactorily explained his connexion with them, our sorrow and our indignation are not unmingled with a sense of humiliation for the discredit that this controversy, under its present aspect, must of necessity throw on the character of English literary men.   It has been no agreeable task for us to take the course we have done; but we cannot but deem it the bounden duty of every man (and more especially of one who by avocation is devoted to the promotion of literature and the establishing of historic truth), at whatever sacrifice, to do his utmost towards setting in their true light a series of demands upon the public credulity, by which, connected as they are with a name of world-wide renown, the unenquiring portion of the literary world might possibly be most seriously misled.